BRITISH
WARSHIPS
& AUXILIARIES
1988/89 Edition

Price
£3.95

THE ROYAL NAVY

A grave question mark now hangs over the future of Britain's defence policy, in particular the nuclear deterrent dependent from the 1990s to at least the year 2025 on the four Trident missile submarines *Vanguard, Victorious, Vengeance* and *Venerable*.

Towards the end of 1987 it became clear from official admissions on both sides of the Atlantic that the latest Russian submarines have achieved "acoustic parity" with those in the British and US fleets. In other words Russian submarines such as the new Akula class nuclear powered attack boats can operate as silently as the latest in the British and US navies.

Submarines were chosen as the vehicles for the British nuclear deterrent because of the invisibility the oceans gave them. It has been said that at no time have the Russians succeeded in tracking one of the Royal Navy's existing Polaris missile submarines on patrol. For a small island there was, too, the advantage that, in the words of an American doggerel of the 1960s:

"Put Polaris out to sea,
Where the real estate is free—
And it's far away from me!"

But senior RN and US Naval officers now admit that Western nuclear submarines can no longer be certain of detecting Russian submarines first. Thus the element of surprise making it possible to get in the first shot in war cannot be relied upon.

Can there be any guarantee in the future that Western Trident submarines will continue to enjoy freedom from detection by Russian hunter-killer submarines? Will they, too, increasingly run the risk of being surprised?

The entry into service of the first RN Trident submarine is still probably five years away. But how far will Russian submarine technology have progressed by then? It is sobering to reflect that as recently as 1983 the then US Chief of Naval Operations in Washington was saying that the Russians' latest submarines' technology was comparable with that of US submarines designed in the 1960s. Yet only four years later the Russians had caught up—largely, it is also officially admitted, thanks to the information they were passed by the "Walker Family" spy ring. These four active and retired US naval officers and ratings, sentenced to long terms of imprisonment in 1986, had been selling the Russians some of the most closely guarded US naval secrets for years.

Almost certainly these included details of the ultra-quiet pump-jet propulsion system used in the RN's latest *Trafalgar* class submarines and likely also to be fitted in the four Trident boats. Details of the pump-jet system had been passed to the US Navy for their new *Seawolf* class submarines at least two years before the spies' arrest in 1985. Little wonder that a senior RN officer, a former nuclear submarine captain, has described the Walkers as "probably the most significant spies to have been caught since 1945".

In 1985, after the spies' arrest, a senior member of the staff of Mr John Lehman, then the US Secretary of the Navy, was asked how the damage they had done Western security could be assessed. He replied: "In 1942, when US General

3

George Patton outsmarted Rommel's Afrika Korps in North Africa, Patton remarked: Rommel, I read your book! That's what the Walkers have allowed the Russians to do: read just how the West would fight a war at sea''.

If the long-term credibility of submarine-launched ballistic missile systems like Trident is in doubt is there an alternative? Certainly the Russians believe so. One of the biggest problems racing the Pentagon today is the growing threat from Russian supersonic submarine-launched cruise missiles against which the space detection systems and weapons of SDI—"Star Wars"—would offer no defence. Such missiles could be launched from almost any of the Russians' latest nuclear powered attack submarines and the fact that two types of such missiles are under development indicates that Moscow puts much store in their future.

Yet in the proposed reduction of medium range nuclear missiles in Europe no mention is made of the Russians' growing submarine cruise missile capability that might well offset any reductions they may be forced to make in land-based cruise missiles.

The Americans, too, have the Tomahawk cruise missile that can be launched from submarines, surface ships or aircraft. As there is no way of telling whether any such vehicles are carrying the nuclear or the high explosive versions of the missile they would pose an enormous problem for the Soviet defences. Equally, it would be impossible to tell if a Russian submarine was carrying nuclear weapons and the assumption must be that virtually all their submarines have nuclear weapons of some sort. In 1981, when a 30 year old Russian "Whisky" class submarine ran aground on the Swedish coast, the Swedes were alarmed to discover its armament included nuclear-tipped torpedoes.

Tomahawk, besides costing far, far less than Trident does not require specially designed submarines to carry it. Thus the submarine capable of launching it need not be confined, like the Trident boats, to a single role, an important factor when numbers of submarines are unlikely ever to match the many requirements for them in peace and war. Such arguments were those of former Navy Minister and Social Democrat Party leader Dr David Owen. That the then Naval Assistant to a former First Sea Lord was among one of the Party's founding members may have some relevance to Dr Owen's proposals.

While this is no place to discuss the merits of any particular political party's proposals there must nonetheless be concern over whether Trident will justify the sacrifices its cost is forcing in other areas of the defence budget. It was chosen in preference to Tomahawk on the grounds of its greatly increased capability to penetrate Russian defences and its 6,000 mile range, compared with 2,500 miles for the existing Polaris, vastly broadened the area in which the Russians would have to seek the submarines. But if there may be no longer any certainty that the submarines will be safe from detection one of the prime arguments in favour of Trident over Tomahawk vanishes.

The attainment of "sonic parity" by the Russians with their latest submarines raises several important issues in anti-submarine warfare.

Warning of any massive surge of Russian submarines from their Northern and Baltic bases depends primarily on the US Sound Surveillance System (SOSUS). This consists of seabed-laid hydrophones linked to shore monitoring stations by cables. Complementing SOSUS, particularly in those areas where it would be politically and militarily impossible to lay fixed seabed installations, will eventually be some 27 US civilian manned auxiliaries equipped with towed array surveillance sonar. Each ship is linked to a shore monitoring station by automatic satellite communications.

Although it has been claimed by some US Navy sources that at least 80 per cent of Russian submarines would have been detected within six hours of the outset of a hot war in the Atlantic such confidenmce will diminish as Russian submarines become harder to detect.

This will mean systems such as SOSUS and shipborne sonars will have to become more and more sensitive to detect the kind of noise which any submarine must make in the course of operating at sea. This irreducible noise minimum stems from such things as that made by the opening or closing of a hull aperture; the operation of a control surface or mast—or the discharge of a weapon.

On a rather longer term reliance will have to be replaced increasingly on active, or transmitting, sonars. Currently such sonars are of short range, compared with detection ranges of 200 miles or more apparently achieved on occasion by the RN's passive towed array sonar ships like the later Type 22 frigates. But unlike the passive, or purely listening, towed array sonar, active sonars can pinpoint and classify an underwater contact, whereas the passive system only indicates the presence and bearing of a contact. The disadvantages in the use of active sonar are limited range and the risk of betrayal of the operating ship's or submarine's presence to an alert enemy.

In the future, perhaps 20 years away, active sonars may achieve ranges comparable to those of towed array passive systems, it is hoped. But to do so they will have to operate at very low frequency and this will mean the operating ship or submarine will have to have a power generating capacity at present not available afloat.

In the mean time, the Western nuclear hunter-killer submarines, with no longer a clear-cut advantage in terms of noise over potential Russian opponents, will have to work increasingly in groups. One submarine may be used as a kind of decoy to lure a hunting Russian submarine to give away its position so that it itself may be surprised and attacked. British and US SSNs are indeed already operating in groups as the surfacing together at the North Pole in spring 1987 of HMS *Superb* and USS *Billfish* and *Sea Devil* demonstrated.

Western submarines will have to rely more on surface ships equipped with long range passive towed array sonar to provide both warning of the presence of hostile submarines and to coordinate the anti-submarine battle along with helicopters and maritime patrol aircraft. Indeed, the role of the towed array sonar equipped surface ship in relation to the friendly submarine has been likened to that of the airborne early-warning aircraft and defending fighters.

In 1981 the proposed cuts in the RN's surface fleet were justified partly on the grounds that frigates had little part to play in the "barrier concept" of patrols by nuclear submarines and shore-based aircraft between Greenland, Iceland and the UK (GIUK) to prevent Russian submarines entering the Atlantic to attack Allied shipping.

But the inclusion of sophisticated surface ships equipped with passive, and in due course possibly active, towed array sonars; and good command and communications facilities to coordinate the efforts of the underwater and air anti-submarine forces is now essential.

Single ships on such patrols, or providing early warning of submarines far ahead of a task group or convoy, would need also to have the means of defending themselves against both air and surface attacks. Their helicopters' prime task would be to keep watch for enemy surface warships and to provide target data for the launching of anti-ship missiles beyond the 30 or so mile radar horizon of the parent ship. It is for this reason that a missile carrying an anti-submarine torpedo would be essential to supplement the helicopter as an anti-submarine weapon carrier. Such a weapon would be a successor to the Australian Ikara missile now in service in only the RN's two surviving Batch I Leanders *Arethusa* and *Euryalus*. Development of such a weapon for the RN was shelved in 1987 for at least two years for economic reasons; as was development of a remotely-controlled ship-operated vehicle able to lay patterns of sonobuoys at high speed. All these requirements add up to a ship that must be much more than just a "cheap and nasty" corvette or beefed up offshore patrol vessel.

With a shrinking budget the Naval Staff inevitably has to concentrate whatever funds are available on building as many first rate frigates as it can. The "Second XI" concept of less capable ships is one that has never appealed for this reason.

Corvettes would be built only to complement, not supplement, the destroyer-frigate force.

The announcement by Mr George Younger, the Secretary of State for Defence, at the Conservative Party conference last October that a further four Type 23 frigates are to be ordered is obviously a welcome move—but must be put in perspective.

In order to maintain a force of 50 operational destroyers and frigates an average annual ordering rate of three ships is required. For this 21 orders should have been placed since the general election in 1979. The actual figure, including the latest four, is 16 of which four are replacements for the four lost in 1982. Not surprisingly some of the *Leander* class frigates will still be in full commission in the second half of the 1990s to maintain numbers at around the present level, which this year will drop to 45. Thus major warships effective lives are perforce being increased from 20 to 25 years.

In September last year (1987), after the Iranian attack on the British registered, Hong Kong owned, tanker *Gentle Breeze*, the Prime Minister was asked by a television reporter if there were plans for further increases in the RN's forces in the Gulf. Ruling out that possibility, she pointed out that there were not the ships available as "you know we have other commitments elsewhere".

That the Prime Minister has recognised the Navy lacks resources may be some encouragement and hopefully she is aware of the problem at least to the extent that her principal naval advisors are prepared to tell her. Whether she is prepared to do anything about it seems less likely since the government's determination to continue curbing its own spending appears unshakable. But some in Britain are beginning once more to realise that trade can be upset by events that in no way reflect economic pressures. Had such pressures played any part in Iran and Iraq the war would have ended years ago. The Iranians in their fanaticism are even resorting to scoring "own goals" with attacks on ships bound for their own ports.

But seven years after the outbreak of the Gulf war there is one encouraging development. This is that co-operation between the Western navies outside the NATO area, hitherto widely viewed as a political impossibility, has become a reality.

The small RN and US Naval forces originally in the Gulf by early last autumn had been joined by warships of the Belgian, Netherlands and Italian navies as well as the French.

Cynics might say that although members of NATO these various nations had acted mainly for reasons of self-interest in that disruption of commercial shipping in the Gulf could seriously damage their economies. Yet membership of any alliance is usually dictated by reasons of self-interest if not self-preservation—but it is nonetheless valid for all that.

For the small Belgian Navy, for example, operating two ocean minesweepers and a support ship in the Gulf must be a major undertaking given its normal practice of seldom deploying outside the North Sea and the Channel, let alone outside the NATO area. The Netherlands' two MCMVs are working as part of the RN MCMV squadron of four Hunt class ships and also rely on the support ship *Abdiel* for spare sweep gear and other stores and for overall command and control of the minesweeping task. Since the Netherlands Navy lacks any MCM support ship the importance of *Abdiel* is further underlined and makes it imperative for her impending scrapping to be reconsidered at least until a proper replacement can be made available. This must, like her, be able to lay exercise and live mines. Yet possible replacements being considered such as the RFA repair ship *Diligence* would have no such capability. It will be interesting to see how a survey ship can fill this role.

The Italian contribution in the Gulf is comparable to that of the RN with three frigates, three MCMVs and two support ships.

The Federal German Navy has sent a number of warships including MCMVs to the Mediterranean to make up for gaps in NATO's strength made by the departure of other Allies' warships to the Gulf. Under the West German constitution their warships may not serve outside the NATO area without special permission of the Bundestag (Parliament).

All of which goes to show what can be ahieved when the politicians at last realise that unpleasant situations do not have a tendency to go away simply by ignoring them.

In 1968 the British government declared that it was no longer the policy to intervene overseas with amphibious operations except with the aid and invovlment of allies. The Falklands War at a stroke invalidated that policy and since then government spokesmen have paid lip service to the need for Britain to retain amphibious forces.

Yet by last autumn question marks were being raised in the press, as so often in the past, over the future of the Royal Marines in the present climate of curbing defence spending. The helicopter carriers (LPH) or Commando ships, vital for strategic flexibility by avoiding dependence upon ports, vanished when the carrier *Hermes* was sold to India and the *Bulwark* scrapped.

Now it seems that their proposed replacements are still-born. Late in 1986 the Defence Ministry's Equipment Procurement Committee approved the earmarking of £200m for two flat-tops, new ships or converted merchantmen, to fulfil the LPH role and for which, later, Mr Younger said there would be a design study. But at the RN Equipment Exhibition at Portsmouth last September senior officers were saying privately that the ASS—Aviation Support Ship as the LPH is now known—had been dropped by the politicians. Only design study contracts have been awarded for modernising or replacing the assault ships *Fearless* and *Intrepid*. Neither they nor any proposed replacements would have the deck spots needed to allow eight helicopters to take off simultaneously carrying 20 men apiece, a company-size lift and the minimum needed in the first wave of an assault to secure a beachhead or helicopter landing zone.

To achieve this in the major amphibious exercise "Purple Warrior" last November the carrier *Illustrious* disembarked her Sea Harriers and was employed as an amphibious helicopter ship carrying a Royal Marines Commando. But it would be very doubtful if one of the carriers could be spared for this task in war.

The Netherlands' as well as the British Marines depend upon the RN's amphibious ships to perform their prime NATO task of making rapid reinforcement of NATO's slender defences in north Norway. Not surprisingly, the abandonment of the ASS project is causing profound concern in NATO circles.

Amphibious operations depend usually upon carriers for air support in the initial stages. So, too, might Western anti-submarine forces since Russian naval leaders have stated they would not make Hitler's mistake and would operate their submarines with air and surface ship support.

To suppose that the Americans' force of 16 operational carriers could meet all the global requirements for air support in war would be dangerously absurd. The RN's three *Invincible* class ships would face innumerable commitments for their eight Sea Harrier fighters, which, as in the Falklands, would likely find themselves doing far more than simply dealing with long-range shore-based shadower aircraft—the task for which they were originally procured.

It is therefore profoundly disturbing that five years after the 1982 conflict, a long time in the life of a front-line aircraft, their modernisation programme, announced officially in 1985, has still not been approved. It will now be quite impossible to complete it by 1990 as had been intended. The number of Sea Harrier pilots is adequate only for peacetime tasks.

With the updating programme for both the Lynx and Sea King helicopters in the pipeline and the new EH-101 helicopter nearing its production stage, in addition to the Sea Harrier modernisation programme, there is surprise and dismay in the Fleet Air Arm that a nuclear submarine engineer should be appointed as the new Director-General Aircraft in the Ministry of Defence in preference to an officer with a naval air engineering background. Just how the officer appointed will be able to talk on equal terms in technical matters with his opposite numbers in the US and elsewhere is far from clear. It appears to show, once again, that some senior officers are unable to grasp that naval air provides the Fleet's prime long-range weapon system today apart from the ballistic missile submarines.

Manpower cuts, ordered in the 1981 Nott Review, continue to bite and just as the South Atlantic commitment was being wound down that in the Gulf has increased. In 1982, before the Review's cuts had really started, the RN had 61,000 officers and men. By next April the total will be 54,900 of whom 49,900 will be fully trained. Further reductions are to come.

Besides greatly increased commitments since 1981 manpower-intensive ships like *Intrepid* and some of the older frigates, which were to have been scrapped, have been retained.

In the words of Capt Nicholas Barker, who commanded *Endurance* in the Falklands War, at a press conference in his new command the new *Sheffield*: "The problem with the Navy is that the commitments are never reduced but the number of ships does not grow. We need 60 destroyers and frigates—we know we won't get them—but it's frustrating because of the enormous spin-off on the domestic front. The consequence is people leave the Service because of separation from wives and families. We have our nose to the grindstone the whole time because we haven't got the tools for the job".

Once such public comments would have been made by some senior serving Admiral and would have attracted widespread notice in the media as a result. That today it falls to a Captain to give a few home truths is perhaps symptomatic of 40 years of peace and the consequent "politicising" of many of the highest appointments in the Service.

Liskeard
Cornwall
December 1987

8

SHIPS OF THE ROYAL NAVY — PENNANT NUMBERS

Ship	Penn. No.	Ship	Penn. No.
Aircraft Carriers		CHARYBDIS	F75
INVINCIBLE	R05	CUMBERLAND	F85
ILLUSTRIOUS	R06	CAMPBELTOWN	F86
ARK ROYAL	R07	CHATHAM	F87
		BROADSWORD	F88
Destroyers		BATTLEAXE	F89
BRISTOL	D23	BRILLIANT	F90
BIRMINGHAM	D86	BRAZEN	F91
NEWCASTLE	D87	BOXER	F92
GLASGOW	D88	BEAVER	F93
EXETER	D89	BRAVE	F94
SOUTHAMPTON	D90	LONDON	F95
NOTTINGHAM	D91	SHEFFIELD	F96
LIVERPOOL	D92	COVENTRY	F98
MANCHESTER	D95	CORNWALL	F99
GLOUCESTER	D96	ROTHESAY	F107
EDINBURGH	D97	PLYMOUTH	F126
YORK	D98	PENELOPE	F127
CARDIFF	D108	AMAZON	F169
		ACTIVE	F171
Frigates		AMBUSCADE	F172
ACHILLES	F12	ARROW	F173
EURYALUS	F15	ALACRITY	F174
DIOMEDE	F16	AVENGER	F185
CLEOPATRA	F28	NORFOLK	F230
ARETHUSA	F38		
SIRIUS	F40	**Submarines**	
PHOEBE	F42	ODIN	S10
MINERVA	F45	OLYMPUS	S12
DANAE	F47	OSIRIS	S13
JUNO	F52	ONSLAUGHT	S14
ARGONAUT	F56	OTTER	S15
ANDROMEDA	F57	ORACLE	S16
HERMIONE	F58	OCELOT	S17
JUPITER	F60	OTUS	S18
APOLLO	F70	OPOSSUM	S19
SCYLLA	F71	OPPORTUNE	S20
ARIADNE	F72	ONYX	S21

Ship	Penn. No.	Ship	Penn. No.
RESOLUTION	S22	BICESTER	M36
REPULSE	S23	CHIDDINGFOLD	M37
RENOWN	S26	ATHERSTONE	M38
REVENGE	S27	HURWORTH	M39
UPHOLDER	S40	BERKELEY	M40
CHURCHILL	S46	QUORN	M41
CONQUEROR	S48	BRERETON	M1113
COURAGEOUS	S50	BRINTON	M1114
TRENCHANT	S91	BRONINGTON	M1115
TALENT	S92	WILTON	M1116
TRIUMPH	S93	CRICHTON	M1124
VALIANT	S102	CUXTON	M1125
WARSPITE	S103	GAVINTON	M1140
SCEPTRE	S104	HUBBERSTON	M1147
SPARTAN	S105	IVESTON	M1151
SPLENDID	S106	KEDLESTON	M1153
TRAFALGAR	S107	KELLINGTON	M1154
SOVEREIGN	S108	KIRKLISTON	M1157
SUPERB	S109	MAXTON	M1165
TURBULENT	S110	NURTON	M1166
TIRELESS	S117	SHERATON	M1181
TORBAY	S118	UPTON	M1187
SWIFTSURE	S126	WALKERTON	M1188
		SOBERTON	M1200
Assault Ships		SANDOWN	M101
FEARLESS	L10	WAVENEY	M2003
INTREPID	L11	CARRON	M2004
		DOVEY	M2005
Minesweepers		HELFORD	M2006
& Minehunters		HUMBER	M2007
BRECON	M29	BLACKWATER	M2008
LEDBURY	M30	ITCHEN	M2009
CATTISTOCK	M31	HELMSDALE	M2010
COTTESMORE	M32	ORWELL	M2011
BROCKLESBY	M33	RIBBLE	M2012
MIDDLETON	M34	SPEY	M2013
DULVERTON	M35	ARUN	M2014

Ship	Penn. No.	Ship	Penn. No.
Patrol Craft		ORKNEY	P299
PEACOCK	P239	LINDISFARNE	P300
PLOVER	P240		
STARLING	P241	**Minelayer**	
SWALLOW	P242	ABDIEL	N21
SWIFT	P243		
SENTINEL	P246	**Survey Ships & RN**	
CORMORANT	P256	**Manned Auxiliaries**	
HART	P257	BRITANNIA	A00
LEEDS CASTLE	P258	GLEANER	A86
REDPOLE	P259	MANLY	A92
KINGFISHER	P260	MENTOR	A94
CYGNET	P261	MILBROOK	A97
PETEREL	P262	MESSINA	A107
SANDPIPER	P263	ROEBUCK	A130
ARCHER	P264	HECLA	A133
DUMBARTON		HECATE	A137
CASTLE	P265	HERALD	A138
BITER	P270	ENDURANCE	A171
SMITER	P272	ETTRICK	A274
PURSUER	P273	ELSING	A277
ANGLESEY	P277	IRONBRIDGE	A311
ALDERNEY	P278	BULLDOG	A317
BLAZER	P279	IXWORTH	A318
DASHER	P280	BEAGLE	A319
ATTACKER	P281	FOX	A320
CHASER	P282	FAWN	A335
FENCER	P283	DATCHET	A357
HUNTER	P284	CHALLENGER	K07
STRIKER	P285		
PUNCHER	P291		
CHARGER	P292		
RANGER	P293		
TRUMPETER	P294	This book is updated and re-issued every *December*. Keep up to date . . . Don't miss the new edition.	
JERSEY	P295		
GUERNSEY	P297		
SHETLAND	P298		

● HMS NEPTUNE

HMS Renown

RESOLUTION CLASS

Ship	Pennant Number	Completion Date	Builder
RESOLUTION	S22	1967	Vickers
REPULSE	S23	1968	Vickers
RENOWN	S26	1968	C. Laird
REVENGE	S27	1969	C. Laird

Displacement 8,400 tons (submerged) **Dimensions** 130m x 10m x 9m **Speed** 25 knots **Armament** 16 Polaris Missiles, 6 Torpedo Tubes **Complement** 147 (x 2).

Notes

These four nuclear-powered Polaris submarines are the United Kingdom's contribution to NATO's strategic nuclear deterrent. At least one of them is constantly on patrol and because of their high speed, long endurance underwater, and advanced sonar and electronic equipment they have little fear of detection.

Each submarine carries 16 Polaris two-stage ballistic missiles, powered by solid fuel rocket motors, 9.45 metres long, 1.37 metres diameter and weighing 12,700 kilogrammes with a range of 2,500 miles. The first of a new Vanguard Class was laid down in December 1986 and the second ordered in October 1987. They will carry the Trident missile.

12

HMS Courageous

VALIANT CLASS

Ship	Pennant Number	Completion Date	Builder
CHURCHILL	S46	1970	Vickers
CONQUEROR	S48	1971	C. Laird
COURAGEOUS	S50	1971	Vickers
VALIANT	S102	1966	Vickers
WARSPITE	S103	1967	Vickers

Displacement 4,900 tons dived **Dimensions** 87m x 10m x 8m **Speed** 28 knots + **Armament** 6 Torpedo Tubes **Complement** 103.

Notes
DREADNOUGHT—the forerunner of this class—is awaiting disposal (by scrap or sinking) at Rosyth. These boats are capable of high underwater speeds and can remain on patrol almost indefinitely. They are able to circumnavigate the world without surfacing. Cost £24-£30 million each to build.

S
U
B
M
A
R
I
N
E
S

● HMS NEPTUNE

HMS Sceptre

SWIFTSURE CLASS

Ship	Pennant Number	Completion Date	Builder
SCEPTRE	S104	1978	Vickers
SPARTAN	S105	1979	Vickers
SPLENDID	S106	1980	Vickers
SOVEREIGN	S108	1974	Vickers
SUPERB	S109	1976	Vickers
SWIFTSURE	S126	1973	Vickers

Displacement 4,500 tons dived **Dimensions** 83m x 10m x 8m **Speed** 30 knots + dived **Armament** 5 Torpedo Tubes **Complement** 116.

Notes
A follow-on class of ships from the successful Valiant Class. These submarines have an updated Sonar and Torpedo system. All are based at Devonport but are slowly being re-deployed to Faslane.

● HMS GANNET

HMS Turbulent

TRAFALGAR CLASS

Ship	Pennant Number	Completion Date	Builder
TRENCHANT	S91	1987	Vickers
TRAFALGAR	S107	1983	Vickers
TURBULENT	S110	1984	Vickers
TIRELESS	S117	1985	Vickers
TORBAY	S118	1986	Vickers
TALENT	S92	Building	Vickers
TRIUMPH	S93	Building	Vickers

Displacement 4,500 tons **Dimensions** 85m x 10m x 8m **Speed** 30+ dived **Armament** 5 Torpedo Tubes **Complement** 125.

Notes
Designed to be considerably quieter than previous submarines. Hull is covered with noise reducing tiles. These boats also have a greater endurance & speed than their predecessors. Cost £200 million + each.

15

VSEL

UPHOLDER CLASS

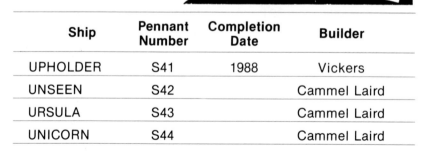

Ship	Pennant Number	Completion Date	Builder
UPHOLDER	S41	1988	Vickers
UNSEEN	S42		Cammel Laird
URSULA	S43		Cammel Laird
UNICORN	S44		Cammel Laird

Displacement 2,400 tons **Dimensions** 70m x 8m x 5m **Speed** 20 knots Dived **Armament** 6 Torpedo Tubes: Sub Harpoon missile **Complement** 44.

Notes

A new class of non-nuclear submarine. The last three named will not be in service until the 1990's. The last of the Porpoise class (SEALION) paid off in 1987. WALRUS is being commercially refitted (1987) to be sold—to Saudi Arabia(?).

16

● HMS NEPTUNE

HMS Odin

OBERON CLASS

Ship	Pennant Number	Completion Date	Builder
ODIN	S10	1962	C. Laird
OLYMPUS	S12	1962	Vickers
OSIRIS	S13	1964	Vickers
ONSLAUGHT	S14	1962	Chatham D'yard
OTTER	S15	1962	Scotts
ORACLE	S16	1963	C. Laird
OCELOT	S17	1964	Chatham D'yard
OTUS	S18	1963	Scotts
OPOSSUM	S19	1964	C. Laird
OPPORTUNE	S20	1964	Scotts
ONYX	S21	1967	C. Laird

Displacement 2,410 tons (submerged) **Dimensions** 90m x 8m x 5m **Speed** 12 knots surface, 17 knots submerged **Armament** 8 Torpedo Tubes **Complement** 70.

Notes
OPOSSUM, OSIRIS & OTTER are fitted with new bow sonars—and others will follow. OBERON paid off for refit and sale—to Saudi Arabia(?) in December 1986. ORPHEUS was reduced to a static training vessel in late 1987.

17

● HMS ILLUSTRIOUS

INVINCIBLE CLASS

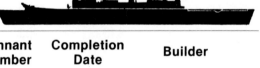

HMS Illustrious

Ship	Pennant Number	Completion Date	Builder
INVINCIBLE	R05	1979	Vickers
ILLUSTRIOUS	R06	1982	Swan-Hunter
ARK ROYAL	R07	1985	Swan-Hunter

Displacement 19,500 tons **Dimensions** 206m x 32m x 6.5m **Speed** 28 knots **Armament** Sea Dart Missile, 2 x 20mm guns, 2 Phalanx **Aircraft** 5 x Sea Harrier, 10 x Sea King **Complement** 900 + aircrews.

Notes
Eventually eight Sea Harriers will be embarked in each ship—but one ship will always be in refit/reserve. INVINCIBLE is currently in long refit at Devonport. Phalanx will be eventually replaced in each ship by the Goalkeeper weapon system during refit periods.

D.J. WALKER

FEARLESS CLASS

HMS Intrepid

Ship	Pennant Number	Completion Date	Builder
FEARLESS	L10	1965	Harland & Wolff
INTREPID	L11	1967	J. Brown

Displacement 12,500 tons, 19,500 tons(flooded) **Dimensions** 158m x 24m x 8m **Speed** 20 knots **Armament** 2 Sea Cat Missile Systems, 2 x 40mm guns, 4 x 30mm + 2 x 20mm (INTREPID only). **Complement** 580.

Notes
Multi-purpose ships that can operate helicopters for embarked Royal Marine Commandos. 4 landing craft are carried on an internal deck and are flooded out when ship docks down. One ship is usually in refit/reserve (currently FEARLESS). Investigations still continue to ascertain if these ships will be replaced or extensively refitted.

19

AIRCRAFT CARRIERS

ASSAULT SHIPS

HMS Bristol

BRISTOL CLASS (Type 82)

Ship	Pennant Number	Completion Date	Builder
BRISTOL	D23	1972	Swan Hunter

Displacement 6,750 tons **Dimensions** 154m x 17m x 7m **Speed** 30 knots + **Armament** 1 x 4.5″ gun, 1 Sea Dart Missile System, 4 x 30mm + 4 x 20mm guns **Complement** 407.

Notes
Four ships of this class were ordered but three later cancelled when requirement for large escorts for fixed wing aircraft carriers ceased to exist. Helicopter Deck provided but no aircraft normally carried. Fitted for, but not with, Vulcan Phalanx. Employed since late 1987 as the Dartmouth Training ship for young officers.

● OFFICIAL PHOTO

HMS Exeter

SHEFFIELD CLASS
(Type 42) Batch 1 & 2

Ship	Pennant Number	Completion Date	Builder
BIRMINGHAM	D86	1976	C. Laird
NEWCASTLE	D87	1978	Swan Hunter
GLASGOW	D88	1978	Swan Hunter
EXETER	D89	1980	Swan Hunter
SOUTHAMPTON	D90	1981	Vosper T.
NOTTINGHAM	D91	1982	Vosper T.
LIVERPOOL	D92	1982	C. Laird
CARDIFF	D108	1979	Vickers

Displacement 3,660 tons **Dimensions** 125m x 15m x 7m **Speed** 29 knots **Armament** 1 x 4.5" gun, 4 x 30mm guns, 4 x 20mm guns, Sea Dart Missile System: Lynx Helicopter. 6 Torpedo Tubes **Complement** 280 +.

Notes
Sister ships SHEFFIELD and COVENTRY lost in 1982 during the Falklands conflict. BIRMINGHAM and EXETER fitted with two Vulcan Phalanx each. SOUTHAMPTON and GLASGOW will be fitted at next refit. The number of 30mm and 20mm guns fitted varies between individual ships.

**D
E
S
T
R
O
Y
E
R
S**

● HMS OSPREY

HMS Manchester

SHEFFIELD CLASS
(Type 42) (Batch 3)

Ship	Pennant Number	Completion Date	Builder
MANCHESTER	D95	1983	Vickers
GLOUCESTER	D96	1984	Vosper T.
EDINBURGH	D97	1985	C. Laird
YORK	D98	1984	Swan Hunter

Displacement 4,775 tons **Dimensions** 132m x 15m x 7m **Speed** 30 knots + **Armament** 1 x 4.5″ gun, 4 x 30mm guns, 4 x 20mm guns Sea Dart missile system. Lynx helicopter, 6 Torpedo Tubes **Complement** 301.

Notes
"Stretched" versions of earlier ships of the class. Extra armament (3 x 30mm weapons) fitted after Falklands crisis—but ships boats had to be removed to provide the space. Ships are designed to provide area air defence of a task force.

HMS Brazen

BROADSWORD CLASS
(Type 22) (Batch 1)

Ship	Pennant Number	Completion Date	Builder
BROADSWORD	F88	1978	Yarrow
BATTLEAXE	F89	1980	Yarrow
BRILLIANT	F90	1981	Yarrow
BRAZEN	F91	1982	Yarrow

Displacement 3,860 tons **Dimensions** 131m x 15m x 6m **Speed** 29 knots **Armament** 4 Exocet Missiles, 2 Sea Wolf Missile Systems, 2 x 40mm guns, 2 or 4 x 20mm guns, 6 Torpedo Tubes, 2 Lynx Helicopters **Complement** 224.

Notes
Planned successor to the Leander Class. Although capable of carrying 2 helicopters, only 1 normally embarked.

FRIGATES

23

HMS Beaver

BROADSWORD CLASS
(Type 22) (Batch 2)

Ship	Pennant Number	Completion Date	Builder
BOXER	F92	1983	Yarrow
BEAVER	F93	1984	Yarrow
BRAVE	F94	1985	Yarrow
LONDON	F95	1986	Yarrow
SHEFFIELD	F96	1987	Swan Hunter
COVENTRY	F98	1988	Swan Hunter

Displacement 4100 tons **Dimensions** 143m x 15m x 6m **Speed** 30 knots **Armament** 4 Exocet Missiles, 2 Sea Wolf Missile Systems, 2 x 40mm + 2 x 20mm guns, 6 Torpedo Tubes, 2 Lynx Helicopters **Complement** 273.

Notes
Ships from BRAVE onwards have enlarged hanger for EH101 helicopter and lightweight Seawolf system. Only 1 helicopter normally embarked.

24

YARROW

HMS Cornwall

BROADSWORD CLASS
(Type 22) (Batch 3)

Ship	Pennant Number	Completion Date	Builder
CUMBERLAND	F85	1988	Yarrow
CAMPBELTOWN	F86	Building	C. Laird
CHATHAM	F87	Building	Swan Hunter
CORNWALL	F99	1987	Yarrow

Displacement 4,200 tons **Dimensions** 147m x 15m x 7m **Speed** 30 knots **Armament** 1 x 4.5″ gun, 1 x Goalkeeper, 8 Harpoon, Seawolf, 4 x 30mm guns, 6 Torpedo Tubes, 2 Lynx or 1 Seaking helicopter **Complement** 250.

Notes
The gun armament & Goalkeeper added to these ships as a result of lessons learnt/re-learnt during the Falklands conflict. All these ships have major A/S capability with their latest towed array sonars. Fitted out as Flag Ships.

● ARTISTS IMPRESSION

HMS Norfolk

DUKE CLASS (Type 23)

Ship	Pennant Number	Completion Date	Builder
NORFOLK	F230	1988/9	Yarrow
MARLBOROUGH	F231	Building	Swan Hunter
ARGYLL	F232	Building	Yarrow
LANCASTER	F233	Building	Yarrow

Displacement 3,500 tons **Dimensions** 133m x 15m x 5m **Speed** 28 knots **Armament** Harpoon & Seawolf missile systems: 1 x 4.5" gun, 4 x 2 twin, magazine launched, Torpedo Tubes **Complement** 157.

Notes

A new generation of cheaper (?) frigate. Costs have more than doubled from initial £67 million quoted. Major problems with ships computer assisted ops room remain to be solved.

S. TALTON

HMS Apollo

LEANDER CLASS

Ship	Pennant Number	Completion Date	Builder
ACHILLES	F12	1970	Yarrow
DIOMEDE	F16	1971	Yarrow
JUNO	F52	1967	Thornycroft
APOLLO	F70	1972	Yarrow
ARIADNE	F72	1972	Yarrow

Displacement 2,962 tons **Dimensions** 113m x 13m x 5m **Speed** 27 knots **Armament** 2 x 4.5″ guns, 3 x 20mm guns, 1 Sea Cat Missile system, 1 Mortar Mk10, 1 Wasp helicopter **Complement** 260.

Notes
JUNO (with a much reduced armament) is a training ship. Most were due to be paid off into reserve but were refitted for further service in the active fleet in the absence of "new build" ships.

DIOMEDE & APOLLO will be paid off in mid '88 and two will be sold overseas. Some ships operate without a helicopter.

HMS Euryalus

LEANDER CLASS (Ikara Conversions)

Ship	Pennant Number	Completion Date	Builder
EURYALUS	F15	1964	Scotts
ARETHUSA	F38	1965	Whites

Displacement 2,860 tons **Dimensions** 113m x 12m x 5m **Speed** 29 knots **Armament** 1 Ikara Anti-submarine Missile, 2 x 40mm guns, 2 Sea Cat Missile Systems, 1 Mortar Mk10, **Complement** 240.

Notes
6 ships were converted (1973-76) to carry the Ikara Anti-submarine Missile System (forward of the bridge) in lieu of a 4.5″ gun. The two remaining are expected to be deleted from the active fleet within the next 2 years. NAIAD paid off in 1987 and is awaiting a new role as a non-seagoing trials vessel at Portsmouth.

HMS Scylla

LEANDER CLASS
(Sea Wolf Conversions)

Ship	Pennant Number	Completion Date	Builder
ANDROMEDA	F57	1968	HM Dockyard Portsmouth
HERMIONE	F58	1969	Stephen
JUPITER	F60	1969	Yarrow
SCYLLA	F71	1970	HM Dockyard Devonport
CHARYBDIS	F75	1969	Harland & Wolff

Displacement 2,962 tons **Dimensions** 113m x 13m x 5m **Speed** 27 knots **Armament** Sea Wolf System, 4 x Exocet Missiles, 2 x 40mm guns, 1 Lynx helicopter **Complement** 260.

Notes
The refitting of these ships cost in the region of £70m—ten times their original cost—but they are now packed with the latest anti-submarine technology. Small calibre armaments vary between individual ships.

29

HMS Danae

LEANDER CLASS
(Exocet Conversions)

Ship	Pennant Number	Completion Date	Builder
● CLEOPATRA	F28	1966	HM Dockyard Devonport
● SIRIUS	F40	1966	HM Dockyard Portsmouth
● PHOEBE	F42	1966	Stephens
MINERVA	F45	1966	Vickers
DANAE	F47	1967	HM Dockyard Devonport
● ARGONAUT	F56	1967	Hawthorn Leslie
PENELOPE	F127	1963	Vickers

Displacement 2,860 tons **Dimensions** 113m x 12m x 5m **Speed** 27 knots **Armament** 4 Exocet Missiles, 3 Sea Cat Missile Systems, 2 x 40mm guns, 6 Torpedo Tubes, 1 Lynx helicopter **Complement** 230.

Notes
The highly successful Leander Class are the last steam powered frigates in the Royal Navy, all later ships being propelled by gas turbines. ● ships have been refitted with Towed Array sonar and their armament reduced to 2 Sea Cat systems. The 40mm guns have been replaced by 20mm weapons to reduce top weight.

HMS Active

AMAZON CLASS (Type 21)

Ship	Pennant Number	Completion Date	Builder
AMAZON	F169	1974	Vosper T.
ACTIVE	F171	1977	Vosper T.
AMBUSCADE	F172	1975	Yarrow
ARROW	F173	1976	Yarrow
ALACRITY	F174	1977	Yarrow
AVENGER	F185	1978	Yarrow

Displacement 3,250 tons **Dimensions** 117m x 13m x 6m **Speed** 30 knots **Armament** 1 x 4.5″ gun, 2 x 20mm guns, 4 Exocet Missiles, 1 Sea Cat Missile System, 1 Lynx helicopter, 6 Torpedo Tubes **Complement** 170.

Notes
These General Purpose frigates were built to a commercial design by Vosper/Yarrow and subsequently sold to the Ministry of Defence. All of the class have been given extra hull strengthening (see photo).

HMS Plymouth

ROTHESAY CLASS (Type 12)

Ship	Pennant Number	Completion Date	Builder
ROTHESAY	F107	1960	Yarrow
PLYMOUTH	F126	1961	HM Dockyard Devonport

Displacement 2,800 tons **Dimensions** 113m x 13m x 5m **Speed** 30 knots **Armament** 2 x 4.5″ guns, up to 4 x 20mm guns, 1 Sea Cat Missile System, 1 Mortar Mk10, 1 Wasp helicopter **Complement** 250.

Notes

Sole survivors of the successful Type 12 Class from which the Leander Class were developed. PLYMOUTH repaired for further service after major fire in 1986. Both are expected to be paid off in 1988.

HMS Cottesmore

MINE COUNTERMEASURES SHIPS (MCMV'S) BRECON CLASS

Ship	Completion Date	Pennant Number	Builder
BRECON	1980	M29	Vosper T.
LEDBURY	1981	M30	Vosper T.
CATTISTOCK	1982	M31	Vosper T.
COTTESMORE	1983	M32	Yarrow
BROCKLESBY	1983	M33	Vosper T.
MIDDLETON	1984	M34	Yarrow
DULVERTON	1983	M35	Vosper T.
BICESTER	1986	M36	Vosper T.
CHIDDINGFOLD	1984	M37	Vosper T.
ATHERSTONE	1987	M38	Vosper T.
HURWORTH	1985	M39	Vosper T.
BERKELEY	1988	M40	Vosper T.
QUORN	1988	M41	Vosper T.

Displacement 625 tonnes **Dimensions** 60m x 10m x 2.2m **Speed** 17 knots **Armament** 1 x 40mm + 2 x 20mm guns **Complement** 45.

Notes

The largest warships ever built of glass reinforced plastic. Designed to replace the Coniston Class—their cost (£35m) has dictated the size of the class. Very sophisticated ships—and lively seaboats! 30mm gun now in COTTESMORE—others will be retro-fitted. 20mm weapons not yet fitted in all ships.

M
C
M
V
E
S
S
E
L
S

G. DAVIES

HMS Ribble

FLEET MINESWEEPERS
RIVER CLASS

Ship	Pennant Number	Completion Date	Builder
WAVENEY	M2003	1984	Richards
CARRON	M2004	1984	Richards
DOVEY	M2005	1984	Richards
HELFORD	M2006	1984	Richards
HUMBER	M2007	1985	Richards
BLACKWATER	M2008	1985	Richards
ITCHEN	M2009	1985	Richards
HELMSDALE	M2010	1985	Richards
ORWELL	M2011	1985	Richards
RIBBLE	M2012	1985	Richards
SPEY	M2013	1985	Richards
ARUN	M2014	1986	Richards

Displacement 850 tons **Dimensions** 47m x 10m x 3m **Speed** 14 knots **Armament** 1 x 40mm, 2 x GPMG **Complement** 30.

Notes

Built as replacements for the MCM ships serving with the RNR. BLACKWATER has an RN ships company and is in the Fishery Protection Squadron (FPS). Built to commercial specifications with steel hulls. Designed for 'sweeping in deep water. Orders for four more of this class were expected in 1987 but were not forthcoming. They are still required for FPS service when finance available.

34

• FLEET PHOTO UNIT

HMS Upton

CONISTON CLASS

Ship	Penn. No.	Ship	Penn. No.
BRERETON (H)	M1113	KIRKLISTON (H) •	M1157
BRINTON (H)	M1114	MAXTON (H)	M1165
BRONINGTON (H)	M1115	NURTON (H)	M1166
WILTON (H)	M1116	SHERATON (H)	M1181
CUXTON (S)	M1125	§UPTON (S)	M1187
GAVINTON (H) •	M1140	WALKERTON (S) •	M1188
HUBBERSTON (H)	M1147	§SOBERTON (S)	M1200
IVESTON (H)	M1151		
KEDLESTON (H)	M1153	• In Reserve at	
KELLINGTON (H)	M1154	Portsmouth	

Displacement 425 tons **Dimensions** 46m x 9m x 3m **Speed** 15 knots **Armament** 1 x 40mm gun, **Complement** 29/38.

Notes
120 of this class were built in the early 50s but most have now been sold overseas or scrapped. They have fulfilled many roles over the years and have given excellent service. WILTON, built of glassfibre in 1973, was the world's first 'plastic' warship. Ships marked § are employed on Coastal Fishery Protection duties. Ships marked (S) are Minesweepers—(H) Minehunters.

35

● ARTISTS IMPRESSION   **HMS Sandown**

SANDOWN CLASS

Ship	Pennant Number	Completion Date	Builder
SANDOWN	M101	1989	Vosper T.
INVERNESS	M102		Vosper T.
CROMER	M103		Vosper T.
WALNEY	M104		Vosper T.
BRIDPORT	M105		Vosper T.

Displacement 450 tons **Dimensions** 53m x 10m x 2m **Speed** 13 knots **Armament** 1 x 30mm gun **Complement** 34.

Notes
A new class designed to operate in deep (continental shelf) waters. Propulsion by vectored thrust and bow thrusters. Plans exist for a further 15 to be built but all the five above will not be in service until 1993.

36

MINELAYER
ABDIEL CLASS

HMS Abdiel

Ship	Pennant Number	Completion Date	Builder
ABDIEL	N21	1967	Thornycroft

Displacement 1,500 tons **Dimensions** 80m x 13m x 4m **Speed** 16 knots **Armament** 44 mines. 1 x 40 mm gun **Complement** 77.

Notes
Designed as a Headquarters and Support Ship for mine counter measure forces and exercise minelayer. Workshops & spares embarked enable minecountermeasures ships to operate well away from home bases.
ABDIEL is the only operational minelayer in the Royal Navy. Due to be paid off, without replacement, early in 1988. Deployed to Gulf in 1987 with extra armament. Due to be relieved as H Q ship in the Gulf by an adapted RN Survey ship (HERALD) in mid '88.

HMS Dumbarton Castle

CASTLE CLASS

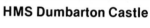

Ship	Pennant Number	Completion Date	Builder
LEEDS CASTLE	P258	1981	Hall Russell
DUMBARTON CASTLE ●	P265	1982	Hall Russell

Displacement 1,450 tons **Dimensions** 81m x 11m x 3m **Speed** 20 knots **Armament** 1 x 40mm gun **Complement** 40.

Notes

These ships have a dual role—that of fishery protection and off-shore patrols within the limits of UK territorial waters. Unlike the Island Class these ships are able to operate helicopters—including Sea King aircraft. Trials have been conducted to assess the suitability of these ships as Minelayers.
● Now in service as a Falkland Island Patrol vessel. LEEDS CASTLE to take over from her sister ship in mid 1988.

HMS Jersey

ISLAND CLASS

Ship	Pennant Number	Completion Date	Builder
ANGLESEY	P277	1979	Hall Russell
ALDERNEY	P278	1979	Hall Russell
JERSEY	P295	1976	Hall Russell
GUERNSEY	P297	1977	Hall Russell
SHETLAND	P298	1977	Hall Russell
ORKNEY	P299	1977	Hall Russell
LINDISFARNE	P300	1978	Hall Russell

Displacement 1,250 tons **Dimensions** 60m x 11m x 4m **Speed** 17 knots **Armament** 1 x 40mm gun **Complement** 39.

Notes
Built on trawler lines these ships were introduced to protect the extensive British interests in North Sea oil installations and to patrol the 200 mile fishery limit.

39

P
A
T
R
O
L

V
E
S
S
E
L
S

PEACOCK CLASS

HMS Peacock

Ship	Pennant Number	Completion Date	Builder
PEACOCK	P239	1983	Hall Russell
PLOVER	P240	1983	Hall Russell
STARLING	P241	1984	Hall Russell
SWALLOW	P242	1984	Hall Russell
SWIFT	P243	1984	Hall Russell

Displacement 700 tons **Dimensions** 60m x 10m x 5m **Speed** 28 knots **Armament** 1 x 76mm gun **Complement** 31.

Notes
The first warships to carry the 76mm Oto Melara gun. They are used to provide an ocean going back-up to the Marine Department of the Hong Kong Police. The Government of Hong Kong has paid 75% of the building and maintenance costs of these vessels. With the run down of forces in the colony the future of two of these ships is "under consideration".

HMS Sentinel

SENTINEL CLASS

Ship	Pennant Number	Completion Date	Builder
SENTINEL	P246	1975	Husumwerft

Displacement 1710 tons **Dimensions** 60m x 13m x 4m **Speed** 14 knots **Armament** 2 x 40mm **Complement** 26.

Notes
Formerly the Oil Rig support vessel Seaforth Saga acquired with PROTECTOR and GUARDIAN (both now sold) for duties as Falkland Island patrol vessels. Returned to UK in '86 for refit but plans for her to return south were abandoned. Replaced WAKEFUL in the Clyde support role in late 1987.

M. LOUAGIE

HMS Biter

COASTAL TRAINING CRAFT
ARCHER CLASS

Displacement 43 tonnes **Dimensions** 20m x 6m x 1m **Speed** 20 knots **Armament** Nil **Complement** 14

Ship	Pennant Number	Completion Date	Builder
ARCHER	P264	1985	Watercraft
BITER	P270	1985	Watercraft
SMITER	P272	1986	Watercraft
PURSUER	P273		
BLAZER	P279		
DASHER	P280		
PUNCHER	P291		
CHARGER	P292		
RANGER	P293		
TRUMPETER	P294		

Notes

For service with RNR divisions and RN University units.

It was announced in 1987 that all 7 ships would be completed, in 1988, by Vosper Thornycroft after original builders liquidation.

• HMS OSPREY

HMS Sandpiper

BIRD CLASS

Ship	Pennant Number	Completion Date	Builder
CORMORANT	P256	1976	James & Stone
HART	P257	1976	James & Stone
REDPOLE	P259	1970	Fairmile
KINGFISHER	P260	1975	R. Dunston
CYGNET	P261	1976	R. Dunston
PETEREL	P262	1976	R. Dunston
SANDPIPER	P263	1977	R. Dunston

Displacement 190 tons **Dimensions** 37m x 7m x 2m **Speed** 21 knots **Armament** 1 x 40mm gun **Complement** 24.

Notes
PETEREL and SANDPIPER are training ships attached to the Britannia Royal Naval College at Dartmouth. REDPOLE, HART and CORMORANT commissioned into the Royal Navy in 1985 after service as RAF search and rescue craft. HART & CORMORANT are smaller craft and are based at Gibraltar.

43

M. LOUAGIE

ATTACKER CLASS

HMS Striker

Ship	Pennant Number	Completion Date	Builder
ATTACKER	P281	1983	Allday
CHASER	P282	1984	Allday
FENCER	P283	1983	Allday
HUNTER	P284	1983	Allday
STRIKER	P285	1984	Allday

Displacement 34 tons **Dimensions** 20m x 5m x 1m **Speed** 24 knots **Complement** 11.

Notes
Seamanship & Navigational training vessels for the Royal Naval Reserve & University RN Units. Based on a successful design used by HM Customs. Ships are based at Glasgow, Aberdeen, Southampton, London and Liverpool respectively.

● RM POOLE

HMS Messina

MANLY CLASS

Ship	Pennant Number	Completion Date	Builder
MANLY	A92	1982	R. Dunston
MENTOR	A94	1982	R. Dunston
MILBROOK	A97	1982	R. Dunston
MESSINA	A107	1982	R. Dunston

Displacement 127 tons **Dimensions** 25m x 6m x 2m **Speed** 10 knots **Complement** 9/13.

Notes
Very similar to the RMAS/RNXS tenders. These four craft are all employed on training duties (first three named attached to HMS RALEIGH for new entry training). MESSINA is a training ship for Royal Marines based at Poole. IXWORTH (A318), ETTRICK (A274), ELSING (A277), IRONBRIDGE (A311) & DATCHET (A357) are all former RMAS tenders now flying the White Ensign.

45

HMS Roebuck

ROEBUCK CLASS

Ship	Pennant Number	Completion Date	Builder
ROEBUCK	A130	1986	Brooke Marine

Displacement 1500 tonnes **Dimensions** 64m x 13m x 4m **Speed** 15 knots **Complement** 47.

Notes
Was due to replace HECLA in the Survey fleet until the latter reprieved in 1987 for further service. Fitted with the latest fixing aids and sector scanning sonar.

HMS Hecate

HECLA CLASS

Ship	Pennant Number	Completion Date	Builder
HECLA	A133	1965	Yarrow
HECATE	A137	1965	Yarrow
HERALD	A138	1974	Robb Caledon

Displacement 2,733 tons **Dimensions** 79m x 15m x 5m **Speed** 14 knots **Complement** 115.

Notes

Able to operate for long periods away from shore support, these ships and the smaller ships of the Hydrographic Fleet collect the data that is required to produce the Admiralty Charts and publications which are sold to mariners worldwide. HERALD is an improved version of the earlier ships and has operated in the South Atlantic in place of HMS Endurance during 1986/7. Plans to dispose of HECLA and HECATE in 1987/8 have been abandoned. HERALD expected to replace ABDIEL (as HQ ship) in the Gulf in early 1988.

47

S
U
R
V
E
Y

S
H
I
P
S

HMS Fox

BULLDOG CLASS

Ship	Pennant Number	Completion Date	Builder
BULLDOG	A317	1968	Brooke Marine
BEAGLE	A319	1968	Brooke Marine
FOX	A320	1968	Brooke Marine
FAWN	A335	1968	Brooke Marine

Displacement 1,088 tons **Dimensions** 60m x 11m x 4m **Speed** 15 knots **Complement** 39.

Notes
Designed to operate in coastal waters. All are to be extensively refitted to extend hull life into the 1990's.
GLEANER (A86) in a small inshore survey craft based at Portsmouth.

HMS London

HMS Argonaut

F56

HMS Brereton

HMS Waveney

HMS Conqueror

HMS Atherstone

M38

RFA Bayleaf

RFA Argus

HMS Challenger

SEABED OPERATIONS VESSEL

Ship	Pennant Number	Completion Date	Builder
CHALLENGER	K07	1984	Scott Lithgow

Displacement 6,400 tons **Dimensions** 134m x 18m x 5m **Speed** 15 knots **Complement** 185.

Notes
CHALLENGER is equipped to find, inspect and, where appropriate, recover objects from the seabed at greater depths than is currently possible. She is designed with a saturation diving system enabling up to 12 men to live in comfort for long periods in a decompression chamber amidships, taking their turns to be lowered in a diving bell to work on the seabed. Also fitted to carry out salvage work. After a series of delays in her construction and acceptance she is expected to become operational in 1988. The "stand in" merchant vessel SEAFORTH CLANSMAN was returned to her owners in mid 1987.

SPECIAL SHIPS

● HMY BRITANNIA

ROYAL YACHT

HMY Britannia

Ship	Pennant Number	Completion Date	Builder
BRITANNIA	A00	1954	J. Brown

Displacement 5,280 tons **Dimensions** 126m x 17m x 5m **Speed** 21 knots **Complement** 250.

Notes
Probably the best known ship in the Royal Navy, BRITANNIA was designed to be converted to a hospital ship in time of war but this conversion was not made during the Falklands crisis. Is available for use in NATO exercises when not on 'Royal' business. Normally to be seen in Portsmouth Harbour when not away on official duties. The only seagoing ship in the RN commanded by an Admiral. Refitted, at Devonport, during 1987.

HMS Endurance

ICE PATROL SHIP

Ship	Pennant Number	Completion Date	Builder
ENDURANCE (ex MV Anita Dan)	A171	1956	Krogerwerft Rendsburg

Displacement 3,600 tons **Dimensions** 93m x 14m x 5m **Speed** 14 knots **Armament** 2 x 20mm guns **Complement** 124.

Notes

Purchased from Denmark in 1967. ENDURANCE is painted brilliant red for easy identification in the ice of Antarctica where she spends 6 months of the year. Her role is to undertake oceanographic and hydrographic surveys in the area and support scientists working ashore. A small Royal Marine detachment is embarked. Was to have been "retired early" after her 1982 season in Antarctica, but reprieved as a result of the Falklands crisis. Refitted at Devonport 1986/7. New flight deck and hangar facilities for 2 Lynx helicopters fitted.

THE NAVY'S MISSILES

SEA SKUA

An anti-surface ship missile. It is carried by the Lynx helicopter.

IKARA

A rocket propelled anti-submarine missile designed to deliver homing torpedoes. It is fitted in two Leander Class frigates.

SEACAT

A close-range anti-aircraft missile. Control is by radar tracking and visual guidance. Propulsion is by solid fuel. It is fitted in older frigates.

SEA DART

A ship-to-air medium-range missile with anti-ship capability. Propulsion is by ramjet and solid boost. It is carried in aircraft carriers and destroyers.

SEA WOLF

A high speed close-range anti-missile and anti-aircraft missile with fully automatic radar control and guidance. It is fitted in some frigates.

EXOCET

A medium-range surface-to-surface missile with a very low trajectory and a radar homing head. It is carried in some frigates.

SIDEWINDER

An infra-red homing air-to-air missile. It has a solid propellant motor and a high explosive warhead. It is carried on the Sea Harrier.

SEA EAGLE

A long-range autonomous sea-skimming anti-ship missile. It is carried on the Sea Harrier.

AS 12

An air-to-surface wire-guided and spin-stabilised missile developed from the SS 11. It has a range of 6,000 metres.

SUB HARPOON

A long-range anti-ship missile launched from a submerged submarine. It is the principal anti-surface ship armament of the Fleet submarines. Harpoon is the "above water version" for later Type 22 and Type 23 frigates.

STING-RAY

The most sophisticated homing torpedo in service. It can be fired from deck-mounted tubes or dropped by helicopter.

POLARIS

Submarine-launched ballistic missile fitted with nuclear warheads. It has a range of 2,500 nautical miles with solid-fuel propulsion.

THE ROYAL FLEET AUXILIARY

The Royal Fleet Auxiliary Service (RFA) is a civilian manned fleet owned and operated by the Ministry of Defence. Its main task is to supply warships of the Royal Navy at sea with fuel, food, stores and ammunition which they need to remain operational while away from base. It also provides aviation support for the Royal Navy together with amphibious support and secure sea transport for Army units and their equipment. The RFA is operated by the Director of Supplies & Transport (Ships and Fuel) whose directorate is one of five that comprise the Royal Naval Supply and Transport service (RNSTS) headed by the Director General Supplies and Transport (Naval).

Today's RFA is very different to what it was even a few years ago. The lessons of the Falkland Islands conflict have not only been learnt but put into practice and are visible in levels of equipment fitted to ships, in new build specifications and in the personnel management of the 2,537 people who comprise the Service.

Besides the normal replenishment roles the Service continues to operate the Forward Repair Ship RFA DILIGENCE. The ship is designed to provide repair and maintenance facilities for both naval and auxiliary vessels which operate away from base ports. After initial employment in the South Atlantic her much needed facilities were deployed to the Gulf in 1987 where she joined two other RFAs in support of naval operations in the area. The charter of her sister ship, STENA SEASPREAD, was extended to meet the Navy's South Atlantic requirements.

The policy of converting selected merchant ships to augment Naval capability and incorporating RFA manning with a substantial Royal naval contingent continues to be highly cost effective. The new Air Training Ship (ATS), RFA ARGUS, like DILIGENCE is an example of this. ARGUS has a total complement of 254 which is made up 79 Royal Fleet Auxiliary personnel, 38 permanent Royal Naval personnel and training detachments of upto 137. On completion of her Part IV trials in 1988 she will replace RFA ENGADINE. ARGUS is, however much more capable; her flight deck is served by two lifts and she has five landing spots. Able to accommodate 6 Sea King helicopters she can transport, but not necessarily operate, 12 Harriers and has a side door giving vehicular access direct from shore.

The Harland and Wolff yard who carried out the conversion of ARGUS have also won the order for the first of the new Auxiliary Oiler Replunishment (AOR) or one stop ships. She is to be named RFA FORT VICTORIA, and is expected to be in service around the end of the decade. She will epitomise the vital role now played by the Service and exemplifies the purposeful, self defended, support ships now being designed to replace the present ageing fleet.

It is however, not only the ships of the RFA that are being streamlined to support the Navy of the nineties. A major manpower study was underway last year to reassess the RFAs requirements in terms of individual skill and overall manning philosophy. This significant reappraisal examined every area of manning activity throughout the fleet. Not only have officers' ranks been retitled but a uniform for the Service's ratings has been specially designed and was worn publicly when the Service was first represented at the 1987 Service of Remembrance.

In training too, higher standards have been achieved. The RFA Service runs its own training for new entry Communication and Supply Officers, and is represented on a wide range of Naval training courses. Ships run the full gauntlet of Operational Sea Training at Portland to ensure they leave Work-up in a high state of operational readiness. Progressively more RFAs are fitted with a defensive capability and gunnery training in RFA ships is going from strength to strength.

The new Landing Ship Logisitic (LSL), RFA SIR GALAHAD, has now been accepted into Service. She was built by Swan Hunter Shipbuilders on the Tyne and will replace the RFA of same name that was tragically lost in the 1982 South Atlantic conflict.

The future status of RFAs is still very much under review and inevitably a move to allow greater flexibility, without altering conditions of service for personnel or deviating from the Department of Transport regulations, will be taken. A few remaining technicalities need to be resolved before a case meeting the RFA requirements is put to Ministers.

A number of merchant ships remain on charter to the MOD—They include MAERSK ASCENSION, MAERSK GANNET, ST BRANDAN, INDOMITABLE, OIL MARINER, NORTHELLA & STENA SEASPREAD. Most are in service in support of the Falkland Island commitment.

SHIPS OF THE ROYAL FLEET AUXILIARY
Pennant Numbers

Ship	Penn. No.		
TIDESPRING	A75	GOLD ROVER	A271
APPLELEAF	A79	BLACK ROVER	A273
BRAMBLELEAF	A81	FORT GRANGE	A385
BAYLEAF	A109	FORT AUSTIN	A386
ORANGELEAF	A110	RESOURCE	A480
OAKLEAF	A111	REGENT	A486
OLWEN	A122	ENGADINE	K08
OLNA	A123	SIR BEDIVERE	L3004
OLMEDA	A124	SIR GALAHAD	L3005
DILIGENCE	A132	SIR GERAINT	L3027
ARGUS	A135	SIR LANCELOT	L3029
GREEN ROVER	A268	SIR PERCIVALE	L3036
GREY ROVER	A269	SIR TRISTRAM	L3505
BLUE ROVER	A270	SIR CARADOC	L3522

RFA Olmeda

'OL' CLASS

Ship	Pennant Number	Completion Date	Builder
OLWEN	A122	1965	Hawthorn Leslie
OLNA	A123	1966	Hawthorn Leslie
OLMEDA	A124	1965	Swan Hunter

Displacement 36,000 tons **Dimensions** 197m x 26m x 10m **Speed** 19 knots **Complement** 108.

Notes
These ships can operate up to 3 Sea King helicopters. Dry stores can be carried—and transferred at sea—as well as a wide range of fuel, aviation spirit and lubricants.

T
A
N
K
E
R
S

63

S. TALTON   RFA Tidespring

TIDE CLASS

Ship	Pennant Number	Completion Date	Builder
TIDESPRING	A75	1963	Hawthorn Leslie

Displacement 27,400 tons **Dimensions** 177m x 22m x 10m **Speed** 18 knots **Complement** 101.

Notes
Built to fuel warships at sea in any part of the world including strengthening for ice operations. A hangar and flight deck provides space for two Sea King helicopters if required. Was due to be "retired early" during 1982/3 but reprieved for Falklands crisis and remains in service but has only a limited career after 25 years service.

ROVER CLASS

RFA Black Rover

Ship	Pennant Number	Completion Date	Builder
GREEN ROVER	A268	1969	Swan Hunter
GREY ROVER	A269	1970	Swan Hunter
BLUE ROVER	A270	1970	Swan Hunter
GOLD ROVER	A271	1974	Swan Hunter
BLACK ROVER	A273	1974	Swan Hunter

Displacement 11,522 tons **Dimensions** 141m x 19m x 7m **Speed** 18 knots **Complement** 49-54.

Notes

Small Fleet Tankers designed to supply HM ships with fresh water, dry cargo and refrigerated provisions as well as a range of fuel and lubricants. Helicopter deck but no hangar.

RFA Oakleaf

LEAF CLASS

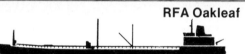

Ship	Pennant Number	Completion Date	Builder
APPLELEAF	A79	1980	Cammell Laird
BRAMBLELEAF	A81	1980	Cammell Laird
BAYLEAF	A109	1982	Cammell Laird
ORANGELEAF	A110	1982	Cammell Laird
OAKLEAF	A111	1981	Uddevalla

Displacement 37,747 tons **Dimensions** 170m x 26m x 12m **Speed** 14.5 knots **Complement** 60.

Notes
All are ex merchant ships either purchased or chartered by MoD. OAKLEAF (ex OKTANIA) differs from the other ships of the class which are all commercial Stat 32 tankers. At 49,310 tons she is the largest vessel in RFA/RN service.

RFA Fort Grange

FORT CLASS

Ship	Pennant Number	Completion Date	Builder
FORT GRANGE	A385	1978	Scott Lithgow
FORT AUSTIN	A386	1979	Scott Lithgow

Displacement 23,384 tons **Dimensions** 183m x 24m x 9m **Speed** 20 knots **Complement** 243, (180 RFA, 18 RNSTS & 45 RN).

Notes
Full hangar and maintenance facilities are provided and up to four Sea King helicopters can be carried for both the transfer of stores and anti-submarine protection of a group of ships. Both can be armed with 2 x 20mm guns mounted on the Scot platforms.

67

STORE SHIPS

● FPS FALKLAND ISLANDS

RFA Regent

REGENT CLASS

Ship	Pennant Number	Completion Date	Builder
RESOURCE	A480	1967	Scotts
REGENT	A486	1967	Harland & Wolff

Displacement 22,890 **Dimensions** 195m x 24m x 8m **Speed** 21 knots **Complement** 182, (RFA 134, RNSTS 37, RN 11).

Notes
The widest range of naval armament stores are carried onboard plus a limited range of general naval stores and food. When the Wessex 5 was withdrawn from service in April 1987 both ships lost their permanently embarked helicopter but they retain full flight deck facilities.

RFA Sir Percivale

LANDING SHIPS
SIR LANCELOT CLASS

Ship	Pennant Number	Completion Date	Builder
SIR BEDIVERE	L3004	1967	Hawthorn
SIR GERAINT	L3027	1967	Stephen
SIR LANCELOT	L3029	1964	Fairfield
SIR PERCIVALE	L3036	1968	Hawthorn
SIR TRISTRAM	L3505	1967	Hawthorn
SIR GALAHAD	L3005	1987	Swan Hunter

Displacement 5,550 tons **Dimensions** 126m x 18m x 4m **Speed** 17 knots **Armament** Can be fitted with 2 x 40mm guns in emergency **Complement** 65, SIR GALAHAD (8,451 tons. 140m x 20m Complement 58.)

Notes
Manned by the RFA but tasked by the Army, these ships are used for heavy secure transport of stores—embarked by bow and stern doors —and beach assault landings. Can operate helicopters from tank deck if required. SIR TRISTRAM was rebuilt at a cost of £13m during 1983-5 as a result of Falklands War damage, a 29′ section being inserted amidships and all aluminium superstructure replaced by steel. SIR GALAHAD entered service in late 1987 replacing the earlier ill fated vessel of the same name.

S. TALTON

RFA Sir Caradoc

Ship	Pennant Number	Completion Date	Builder
SIR CARADOC	L3522	1973	Trosvik Verksted

Displacement 3,350 tons **Dimensions** 124m x 16 **Speed** 14 knots **Complement** 24

Notes

Chartered as a stop gap replacement for former RFA SIR GALAHAD.

Found to be unsuitable for the South Atlantic and mainly employed on the Marchwood/Antwerp freight run for MoD (Army) will be returned to her owners once the new SIR GALAHAD is fully operational.

● HMS OSPREY

RFA Diligence

Ship	Pennant Number	Completion Date	Builder
DILIGENCE	A132	1981	Oresundsvarvet

Displacement 5,814 tons **Dimensions** 120m x 12m **Speed** 15 knots
Complement RFA 40. RN Personnel — approx 100.

Notes
Formerly the M/V Stena Inspector purchased (£25m) for service in the South Atlantic. Accommodation is provided for a 100 man Fleet Maintenance Unit. Her deep diving complex has been removed & workshops added. Refitted in UK during 1987 and returned to the Falklands. Deployed to Oman to support RN ships operating in the Gulf in late 1987.

RFA Argus

Ship	Pennant Number	Completion Date	Builder
ARGUS	A135	1981	Cantieri Navali Breda

Displacement 28,081 tons (full load) **Dimensions** 175m x 30m x 8m **Speed** 18 knots **Armament** 4 x 30mm. 2 x 20mm **Complement** 254 (inc 137 Air Group) **Aircraft** 6 Sea King, 12 Harriers can be carried in a "ferry role".

Notes
Formerly the M/V CONTENDER BEZANT taken up from trade during the Falklands crisis. Purchased in 1984 (£13 million) for conversion to an 'Aviation Training Ship'. A £50 million re-build was undertaken at Belfast from 1984-87. After she has completed her extensive Part IV trials she will replace ENGADINE and operate from Portland.

RFA Engadine

Ship	Pennant Number	Completion Date	Builder
ENGADINE	K08	1967	Robb

Displacement 9000 tons **Dimensions** 129m x 17m x 7m **Speed** 16 knots **Complement** 175 (73 RFA + up to 102 RN personnel).

Notes

Specially built for RFA service (but with embarked RN personnel) to provide training ship for helicopter crews operating in deep waters well away from coasts. Can operate up to 4 Sea Kings or 5 Lynx and often embarks pilotless target aircraft for exercises. Due to be deleted from the RFA list in mid 1988 but a secondary further role may be found for her.

ROYAL MARITIME AUXILIARY SERVICE

The Royal Maritime Auxiliary Service Fleet is comprised of over 500 hulls, of which 310 are self propelled, including small harbour launches, the remainder being dumb craft such as lighters etc. It is administered by the Director of Marine Services (Naval) to whom the Captains of the Ports and Resident Naval Officers at the various Naval Bases are mainly responsible for the provision of Marine Services to the Royal Navy. The RMAS also provides many types of craft for the numerous and diverse requirements of other Ministry of Defence departments.

Ships of the RMAS, which can be seen at work in all the Naval Bases throughout the United Kingdom and at Gibraltar, are easily identified by their black hulls, buff coloured superstructure and funnels, and by the RMAS flag, which is a blue ensign defaced in the fly by a yellow anchor over two wavy lines. Pennant numbers are painted only on those vessels that are normally employed outside harbour limits.

● A. MASON   **Dog Class Tugs in formation at Faslane**

The largest section of the fleet is employed on harbour duties, the types of vesels involved being Berthing and Tractor Tugs, Fleet Tenders, Tank Cleaning Lighters, Harbour Launches, Naval Armament Vessels and dumb lighters for carrying explosive stores, general stores, fuel, water and victuals to the Royal Navy, NATO Navies and Royal Fleet Auxiliary ships when they are in port or at anchor. In keeping with the Director of Marine Services policy of multi-role vessels, many of the larger units of the fleet have been modified to back up the harbour fleet when required.

A smaller section of the fleet is, however, engaged in a purely sea-going capacity. Ocean Tugs, Torpedo Recovery Vessels and Mooring and Salvage Vessels are designed and equipped for world wide towing and complex Marine Salvage operations. Experimental Trials Vessels, fitted with some of the most sophisticated modern equipment, are deployed on a wide range of duties in the fast growing area of advanced experimental technology necessary for the design of new warships, weapon systems and machinery.

Problems associated with the control and treatment of oil pollution at sea have become more pressing in recent years. To deal with emergencies in Dockyard Ports and to assist the Department of Transport with those that may arise around the coastline of the United Kingdom, the RMAS has adapted many of its vessels to carry chemical dispersants and the necessary spraying equipent. A review is underway however to ascertain if it would be more cost-effective for this task to be carried out by commercial contractors.

The size and composition of the RMAS Fleet is under constant review to ensure its compatibility with the changing requirements of the Royal Navy, which it exists to serve. Older units are being phased out, at times without replacement, and the introduction of new more versatile vessels will continue to provide savings in the total number of ships required and the manpower required to operate them.

Pressure has increased over recent years in all areas of Defence Expenditure to obtain the best possible value for money in the interests of maintaining "the teeth" at maximum efficiency. It is inevitable therefore that much of the pressure falls upon the support area in which the Marine Services play a vital part.

Reviews into the future composition/role of the various parts of RMAS have still not been complete. Manpower on many of its vessels have been reduced—with the very real fear of commercial vessels taking over many of the traditional roles the service has undertaken.

At the end of the day it looks as if all the audits/reviews have kept a lot of "investigators" occupied, & typists busy but at the end of the day not a lot will be seen to change.

However, it should be stated that the professional standards achieved by the Marine Services are second to none, and are held in high regard by all its customers. The chief concern of DMS(N) is to preserve the services provided to the Fleet and his other customers in the most cost effective way and without loss of operational flexibility. Not an easy task in days of financial restraint. If however more monies can be found for the front line Fleet all the 'reviews' will have been worthwhile.

SHIPS OF THE ROYAL MARITIME AUXILIARY SERVICE —
PENNANT NUMBERS

Ship	Penn. No.	Ship	Penn. No.
MELTON	A83	LABRADOR	A168
MENAI	A84	KITTY	A170
MEON	A87	LESLEY	A172
MILFORD	A91	DOROTHY	A173
TYPHOON	A95	LILAH	A174
BEMBRIDGE	A101	MARY	A175
ALSATIAN	A106	EDITH	A177
FELICITY	A112	HUSKY	A178
MAGNET	A114	MASTIFF	A180
LODESTONE	A115	IRENE	A181
CAIRN	A126	SALUKI	A182
TORRENT	A127	ISABEL	A183
TORRID	A128	SALMOOR	A185
DALMATION	A129	SALMASTER	A186
TORNADO	A140	SALMAID	A187
TORCH	A141	POINTER	A188
TORMENTOR	A142	SETTER	A189
TOREADOR	A143	JOAN	A190
DAISY	A145	JOYCE	A193
WATERMAN	A146	GWENDOLINE	A196
FRANCES	A147	SEALYHAM	A197
FIONA	A148	HELEN	A198
FLORENCE	A149	MYRTLE	A199
GENEVIEVE	A150	SPANIEL	A201
GEORGINA	A152	NANCY	A202
EXAMPLE	A153	NORAH	A205
EXPLORER	A154	LLANDOVERY	A207
DEERHOUND	A155	LAMLASH	A208
DAPHNE	A156	CHARLOTTE	A210
LOYAL HELPER	A157	LECHLADE	A211
SUPPORTER	A158	ENDEAVOUR	A213
LOYAL WATCHER	A159	BEE	A216
LOYAL VOLUNTEER	A160	CHRISTINE	A217
LOYAL MEDIATOR	A161	LOYAL MODERATOR	A220
ELKHOUND	A162		
EXPLOIT	A163	FORCEFUL	A221
GOOSANDER	A164	NIMBLE	A222
POCHARD	A165	POWERFUL	A223
KATHLEEN	A166	ADEPT	A224
EXPRESS	A167	BUSTLER	A225

Ship	Penn. No.	Ship	Penn. No.
CAPABLE	A226	GLENCOE	A392
CAREFUL	A227	DUNSTER	A393
FAITHFUL	A228	FINTRY	A394
CRICKET	A229	GRASMERE	A402
COCKCHAFER	A230	KINLOSS	A482
DEXTEROUS	A231	CROMARTY	A488
GNAT	A239	DORNOCH	A490
SHEEPDOG	A250	ROLLICKER	A502
LYDFORD	A251	HEADCORN	A1766
DORIS	A252	HEVER	A1767
LADYBIRD	A253	HARLECH	A1768
MEAVEY	A254	HAMBLEDON	A1769
CICALA	A263	LOYAL	
SCARAB	A272	CHANCELLOR	A1770
KINBRACE	A281	LOYAL PROCTOR	A1771
AURICULA	A285	HOLMWOOD	A1772
ILCHESTER	A308	HORNING	A1773
INSTOW	A309	MANDARIN	P192
FOXHOUND	A326	PINTAIL	P193
BASSET	A327	GARGANEY	P194
COLLIE	A328	GOLDENEYE	P195
CORGI	A330	ALNMOUTH	Y13
FOTHERBY	A341	WATERFALL	Y17
FELSTEAD	A348	WATERSHED	Y18
CARTMEL	A350	WATERSPOUT	Y19
ELKSTONE	A353	WATERSIDE	Y20
FROXFIELD	A354	OILPRESS	Y21
EPWORTH	A355	OILSTONE	Y22
ROYSTERER	A361	OILWELL	Y23
DOLWEN	A362	OILFIELD	Y24
DENMEAD	A363	OILBIRD	Y25
WHITEHEAD	A364	OILMAN	Y26
FULBECK	A365	WATERCOURSE	Y30
ROBUST	A366	WATERFOWL	Y31
NEWTON	A367		
KINTERBURY	A378		
THROSK	A379		
CRICKLADE	A381		
CLOVELLY	A389		
CRICCIETH	A391		

SKYFOTOS

RMAS Rollicker

ROYSTERER CLASS

Ship	Pennant Number	Completion Date	Builder
ROYSTERER	A361	1972	C.D. Holmes
ROBUST	A366	1974	C.D. Holmes
ROLLICKER	A502	1973	C.D. Holmes

G.R.T. 1,036 tons **Dimensions** 54m x 12m x 6m **Speed** 15 knots **Complement** 21.

Notes
Built for salvage and long range towage, but are frequently used for various "deepwater" trials.

78

M. LENNON

RMAS Typhoon

TYPHOON CLASS

Ship	Pennant Number	Completion Date	Builder
TYPHOON	A95	1960	Henry Robb

G.R.T. 1,034 tons **Dimensions** 60m x 12m x 4m **Speed** 17 knots **Complement** 27.

Notes
Long range towage and salvage tug. Now laid up, at Portsmouth, in reserve.

W. SARTORI

RMAS Bustler

HARBOUR TUGS
TWIN UNIT TRACTOR TUGS (TUTT'S)

Ship	Pennant Number	Completion Date	Builder
FORCEFUL	A221	1985	R. Dunston
NIMBLE	A222	1985	R. Dunston
POWERFUL	A223	1985	R. Dunston
ADEPT	A224	1980	R. Dunston
BUSTLER	A225	1981	R. Dunston
CAPABLE	A226	1981	R. Dunston
CAREFUL	A227	1982	R. Dunston
FAITHFUL	A228	1985	R. Dunston
DEXTEROUS	A231	1986	R. Dunston

G.R.T. 375 tons **Dimensions** 39m x 10m x 4m **Speed** 12 knots
Complement 9

Notes
The principle harbour tug in naval service. CAPABLE is at
Gibraltar.

RMAS Alsatian

DOG CLASS

Ship	Penn. No.	Ship	Penn. No.
ALSATIAN	A106	POINTER	A188
CAIRN ●	A126	SETTER	A189
DALMATIAN	A129	SEALYHAM	A197
DEERHOUND	A155	SPANIEL	A201
ELKHOUND	A162	SHEEPDOG	A250
LABRADOR	A168	FOXHOUND	A326
HUSKY	A178	BASSET	A327
MASTIFF	A180	COLLIE ●	A328
SALUKI	A182	CORGI	A330

G.R.T. 152 tons **Dimensions** 29m x 8m x 4m **Speed** 12 knots **Complement** 5

Notes
General harbour tugs — all completed between 1962 & 1972.
● No longer tugs. Refitted as trials vessels for service at Kyle of Lochalsh.
A new (commercial) tug is expected to be hired for a short period to evaluate the 'Z' Drive Concept as a possible propulsion system for a new class of medium berthing tugs.

W. SARTORI

RMAS Dorothy

IMPROVED GIRL CLASS

Ship	Penn. No.	Ship	Penn. No.
DAISY	A145	CHARLOTTE	A210
DAPHNE	A156	CHRISTINE	A217
DOROTHY	A173	DORIS	A252
EDITH	A177		

G.R.T. 75 tons **Speed** 10 knots **Complement** 4

Notes
All completed 1971-2.

RMAS Kathleen

IRENE CLASS

Ship	Penn. No.	Ship	Penn. No.
KATHLEEN	A166	ISABEL	A183
KITTY	A170	JOAN	A190
LESLEY	A172	JOYCE	A193
LILAH	A174	MYRTLE	A199
MARY	A175	NANCY	A202
IRENE	A181	NORAH	A205

G.R.T. 89 tons **Speed** 8 knots **Complement** 4

Notes

Known as Water Tractors these craft are used for basin moves and towage of light barges.

RMAS Helen

FELICITY CLASS

Ship	Penn. No.	Ship	Penn. No.
FELICITY	A112	GENEVIEVE	A150
FRANCES	A147	GEORGINA	A152
FIONA	A148	GWENDOLINE	A196
FLORENCE	A149	HELEN	A198

G.R.T. 80 tons **Speed** 10 knots **Complement** 4

Notes
Water Tractors — completed in 1973; FRANCES, FLORENCE & GENEVIEVE completed 1980.

M. LENNON

RMAS Whitehead

TRIALS SHIPS

Ship	Pennant Number	Completion Date	Builder
WHITEHEAD	A364	1971	Scotts

G.R.T. 3,427 tons **Dimensions** 97m x 15m x 5m **Speed** 15.5 knots **Complement** 38

Notes
Fitted with Torpedo Tubes for trial firings. Long term future under discussion within MoD. No longer fully employed as a Torpedo trials vessel and a decision regarding the viability of a mid-life refit is awaited.

85

M. LENNON

RMAS Newton

Ship	Pennant Number	Completion Date	Builder
NEWTON	A367	1976	Scotts

G.R.T. 2,779 tons **Dimensions** 99m x 16m x 6m **Speed** 15 knots **Complement** 39

Notes
Built as sonar propagation trials ship but can also be used as a Cable Layer.

M. LENNON

RMAS Auricula

TEST & EXPERIMENTAL SONAR TENDER

Ship	Pennant Number	Completion Date	Builder
AURICULA	A285	1981	Ferguson Bros

G.R.T. 981 tons **Dimensions** 52m x 11m x 3m **Speed** 12 knots
Complement 20

Notes
Employed on evaluation work of new sonar equipment that may equip RN ships of the future. Based at Portland.

M. LENNON

RMAS Throsk

ARMAMENT STORES CARRIERS

Ship	Pennant Number	Completion Date	Builder
KINTERBURY	A378	1980	Appledore SB
THROSK	A379	1977	Cleland SB Co.

G.R.T. 1,357 tons **Dimensions** 64m x 12m x 5m **Speed** 14 knots **Complement** 19

Notes
2 holds carry Naval armament stores, ammunition and guided missiles. KINTERBURY varies slightly from earlier sister ship. One ship is normally operational—the other in reserve. The Army's Armament Stores Carrier ST GEORGE is very similar.

M. LENNON

RMAS Scarab

INSECT CLASS

Ship	Pennant Number	Completion Date	Builder
BEE	A216	1970	C.D. Holmes
CRICKET	A229	1972	Beverley
COCKCHAFER	A230	1971	Beverley
GNAT	A239	1972	Beverley
LADYBIRD	A253	1973	Beverley
CICALA	A263	1971	Beverley
SCARAB	A272	1973	Beverley

G.R.T. 279 tons **Dimensions** 34m x 8m x 3m **Speed** 10.5 knots
Complement 7-9

Notes
CRICKET and SCARAB are fitted as Mooring Vessels and
COCKCHAFER as a Trials Stores Carrier — remainder are Naval
Armament carriers.

T
E
N
D
E
R
S

M. LENNON   **RNXS Loyal Helper**

LOYAL CLASS

Ship	Penn. No.	Ship	Penn. No.
LOYAL HELPER	A157	LOYAL MEDIATOR	A161
SUPPORTER	A158	LOYAL MODERATOR	A220
LOYAL WATCHER	A159	LOYAL CHANCELLOR	A1770
LOYAL VOLUNTEER	A160	LOYAL PROCTOR	A1771

G.R.T. 112 tons **Dimensions** 24m x 6m x 3m **Speed** 10.5 knots
Complement 24

Notes
All these craft are operated by the Royal Naval Auxiliary Service
(RNXS) — men (and women) — who in time of emergency would
man these craft for duties as port control vessels.

AUTHOR'S PHOTO

RMAS Llandovery

(TYPE A, B & X) TENDERS

Ship	Penn. No.	Ship	Penn. No.
MELTON	A83	FULBECK	A365
MENAI	A84	CRICKLADE	A381
MEON	A87	CLOVELLY	A389
MILFORD	A91	CRICCIETH	A391
LLANDOVERY	A207	GLENCOE	A392
LAMLASH	A208	DUNSTER	A393
LECHLADE	A211	FINTRY	A394
LYDFORD	A251	GRASMERE	A402
MEAVEY	A254	CROMARTY	A488
ILCHESTER*	A308	DORNOCH	A490
INSTOW*	A309	HEADCORN	A1766
FOTHERBY	A341	HEVER	A1767
FELSTEAD	A348	HARLECH	A1768
ELKSTONE	A353	HAMBLEDON	A1769
FROXFIELD	A354	HOLMWOOD	A1772
EPWORTH	A355	HORNING	A1773
DENMEAD	A363		

G.R.T. 78 tons **Dimensions** 24m x 6m x 3m **Speed** 10.5 knots **Complement** 4/5

Notes
All completed since 1971 to replace Motor Fishing Vessels. Vessels marked* are diving tenders. Remainder are Training Tenders, Passenger Ferries, or Cargo Vessels. GLENCOE is on loan to the RNXS—based at Portsmouth—and painted grey.

M. LENNON

RMAS Alnmouth

ABERDOVEY CLASS ('63 DESIGN)

Ship	Penn. No.	Ship	Penn. No.
ALNMOUTH	Y13	CARTMEL	A350
BEMBRIDGE	A101		

G.R.T. 77 tons **Dimensions** 24m x 5m x 3m **Speed** 10.5 knots **Complement** 4/5

Notes
ALNMOUTH is a Sea Cadet Training Ship based at Plymouth, BEMBRIDGE at Portsmouth. CARTMEL is on loan to the RNXS based on the Clyde. Other vessels of the class now used by Sea Cadet/RNR Units. BEAULIEU and BLACKENEY sold to Falkland Island Government.

● HMS DAEDALUS

XSV Example

COASTAL TRAINING CRAFT
EXAMPLE CLASS

Ship	Pennant Number	Completion Date	Builder
XSV EXAMPLE	A153	1985	Watercraft
XSV EXPLORER	A154	1985	Watercraft
XSV EXPLOIT	A163		Vosper T
XSV EXPRESS	A167	1988	Vosper T

Displacement 43 tons **Dimensions** 20m x 6m x 1m **Speed** 20 knots
Armament Nil **Complement** 14

Notes
Should have replaced the former Inshore Minesweepers in RNXS
service, but the arrival of the last two delayed by the collapse of
original builders. EXPRESS to complete in 1988—EXPLOIT a year
later. PORTISHAM (lms) undergoing repairs for further service.

RMAS Oilstone

OILPRESS CLASS

Ship	Pennant Number	Completion Date	Builder
OILPRESS	Y21	1969	Appledore Shipbuilders
OILSTONE	Y22	1969	" "
OILWELL	Y23	1969	" "
OILFIELD	Y24	1969	" "
OILBIRD	Y25	1969	" "
OILMAN	Y26	1969	" "

G.R.T. 362 tons **Dimensions** 41m x 9m x 3m **Speed** 11 knots **Complement** 5

Notes
Employed as Harbour and Coastal Oilers. OILFIELD is in reserve at Portsmouth.

W. SARTORI

RMAS Waterman

WATER CARRIERS
WATER CLASS

Ship	Pennant Number	Completion Date	Builder
WATERFALL	Y17	1967	Drypool Eng Co
WATERSHED	Y18	1967	Drypool Eng Co
WATERSPOUT	Y19	1967	Drypool Eng Co
WATERSIDE	Y20	1968	Drypool Eng Co
WATERCOURSE	Y30	1974	Drypool Eng Co
WATERFOWL	Y31	1974	Drypool Eng Co
WATERMAN	A146	1978	R. Dunston

G.R.T. 263 tons **Dimensions** 40m x 8m x 2m **Speed** 11 knots
Complement 5

Notes
Capable of coastal passages, these craft normally supply either demineralised or fresh water to the Fleet within port limits.

RMAS Magnet

DEGAUSSING VESSELS
MAGNET CLASS

Ship	Pennant Number	Completion Date	Builder
MAGNET	A114	1979	Cleland
LODESTONE	A115	1980	Cleland

G.R.T. 828 tons **Dimensions** 55m x 12m x 4m **Speed** 14 knots
Complement 9

Notes
One ship is normally operational, the other kept in reserve.

RMAS Torrid

TORPEDO RECOVERY VESSELS (TRV'S)
TORRID CLASS

Ship	Pennant Number	Completion Date	Builder
TORRENT	A127	1971	Cleland SB Co
TORRID	A128	1972	Cleland SB Co

G.R.T. 550 tons **Dimensions** 46m x 9m x 3m **Speed** 12 knots
Complement 14

Notes
A stern ramp is built for the recovery of torpedoes fired for trials
and exercises. A total of 32 can be carried.

T
R
V
's

97

RMAS Tornado

TORNADO CLASS

Ship	Pennant Number	Completion Date	Builder
TORNADO	A140	1979	Hall Russell
TORCH	A141	1980	Hall Russell
TORMENTOR	A142	1980	Hall Russell
TOREADOR	A143	1980	Hall Russell

G.R.T. 560 tons **Dimensions** 47m x 8m x 3m **Speed** 14 knots
Complement 13

Notes
TORCH is based at Portland, TORMENTOR at Plymouth —
remainder on the Clyde.

W. SARTORI

RMAS Salmoor

SAL CLASS

Ship	Pennant Number	Completion Date	Builder
SALMOOR	A185	1985	Hall Russell
SALMASTER	A186	1986	Hall Russell
SALMAID	A187	1986	Hall Russell

Displacement 2200 tonnes **Dimensions** 77m x 15m x 4m **Speed** 15 knots **Complement** 17

M S V 's

Notes
Built at a cost of £9 million each these ships have replaced the 40-year-old Kin class. They are multi-purpose vessels designed to lay and maintain underwater targets and moorings and undertake a wide range of salvage tasks.

AUTHOR'S PHOTO

RMAS Goosander

WILD DUCK CLASS

Ship	Pennant Number	Completion Date	Builder
MANDARIN	P192	1964	C. Laird
PINTAIL	P193	1964	C. Laird
GARGANEY	P194	1966	Brooke Marine
GOLDENEYE	P195	1966	Brooke Marine
GOOSANDER	A164	1973	Robb Caledon
POCHARD	A165	1973	Robb Caledon

G.R.T. 900 tons* **Dimensions** 58mm x 12m x 4m **Speed** 10 knots
Complement 18
* Vessels vary slightly

Notes
Vessels capable of carrying out a wide range of duties laying moorings and heavy lift salvage work. 200 tons can be lifted over over the bow. MANDARIN is in reserve at Portsmouth.

100

RMAS Kinloss

KIN CLASS

Ship	Pennant Number	Completion Date	Builder
KINBRACE	A281	1944	A. Hall Aberdeen
KINLOSS	A482	1945	A. Hall Aberdeen

Displacement 1,050 tons **Dimensions** 54m x 11m x 4m **Speed** 9 knots **Complement** 18

Notes
Coastal Salvage Vessels re-engined between 1963 & 1967. KINBRACE is now in reserve at Portsmouth and KINLOSS has a trials role at Rosyth.

RMAS Dolwen

DOLWEN CLASS

Ship	Pennant Number	Completion Date	Builder
DOLWEN (ex Hector Gulf)	A362	1962	P.K. Harris

Displacement 602 tons **Dimensions** 41m x 9m x 4m **Speed** 14 knots **Complement** 11

Notes
Built as a stern trawler, then purchased for use as a Buoy tender — now used as a Range Mooring Vessel for RAE ABERPORTH (S. Wales) from her base at Pembroke Dock. Negotiations with Scott Lithgow to build a replacement vessel collapsed in late 1987 and another yard will now build the vessel—it will probably be named WARDEN.

HMAV Ardennes

ARMY LANDING CRAFT

LCL CLASS   LANDING CRAFT LOGISTIC

Vessel	Pennant Number	Completion Date	Builder
HMAV Ardennes	L4001	1977	Brooke Marine
HMAV Arakan	L4003	1978	Brooke Marine

Displacement 1,050 tons **Dimensions** 72m x 15m x 2m **Speed** 10 knots **Complement** 36

Notes
Designed to carry up to 520 tonnes of cargo, overside loaded, or up to Five Chieftain tanks—Ro Ro loaded, reducing to 254 tonnes for beaching operations, through bow doors. Principal roles are maintenance of the Royal Artillery Range Outer Hebrides and in support of Amphibious Operations and Exercises.

103

M. LOUAGIE

RCTV Andalsnes

RCL CLASS

RAMPED CRAFT LOGISTIC

Vessel	Pennant Number	Completion Date	Builder
RCTV Arromanches	L105	1981	Brooke Marine
RCTV Antwerp	L106	1981	Brooke Marine
RCTV Andalsnes	L107	1984	James & Stone
RCTV Abbeville	L108	1985	James & Stone
RCTV Akyab	L109	1985	James & Stone
RCTV Aachen	L110	1986	McTay Marine
RCTV Arezzo	L111	1986	McTay Marine
RCTV Agheila	L112	1987	McTay Marine
RCTV Audemer	L113	1987	McTay Marine

Displacement 165 tons **Dimensions** 30m x 8m x 2m **Speed** 9 knots **Complement** 6

Notes
Smaller—"all purpose" landing craft capable of carrying up to 100 tons. In service in coastal waters around Cyprus, Hong Kong & UK.

AIRCRAFT OF THE FLEET AIR ARM

British Aerospace Sea Harrier

Variants: FRS 1 (FRS 2 undergoing development 1988/89)
Role: Short take off, vertical landing (STOVL) fighter, reconnaissence and strike aircraft.
Engine: 1 x 21,500lb thrust Rolls Royce PEGASUS 104 turbojet.
Span 25'3" **length** 47'7" **height** 12'0" **max weight** 26,200lb.
Max speed Mach 1.2 **Crew** 1 pilot.
Avionics: Blue Fox pulse radar. (To be replaced by the Blue Vixen pulse doppler radar in the FRS 2).
Armament: SEA EAGLE air to surface missiles. SIDEWINDER air to air missiles. (FRS 2 to carry the new Anglo/US AMRAAM radar guided air to air missiles). 2 x 30mm Aden cannons with 120 rounds per gun in detachable pods, one either side of the lower fuselage. 1 fuselage centreline and 4 underwing hardpoints. The inner wing stations are capable of carrying 2,000lb of stores and are plumbed for drop tanks. The other positions can carry stores up to 1,000lb in weight. Possible loads include 1,000lb, 500lb or practice bombs; BL 755 cluster bombs, Lepus flares, 190 or 100 gallon drop tanks. A single F95 camera is mounted obliquely in the nose for the reconnaissence role.
Squadron Service: 800, 801 and 899 squadrons in commission.
Notes: During 1988, 800 squadron will be embarked in HMS ILLUSTRIOUS and 801 in HMS ARK ROYAL. 899 squadron is responsible for the training of replacement pilots and the development of tactics and is normally shore based at RNAS YEOVILTON. In a period of tension it could embark to reinforce the embarked air groups in the carriers.

Westland SEA KING

Developed for the Royal Navy from the Sikorsky SH3D, the basic Seaking airframe is used in three different roles. The following details are common to all:
Engines 2 x 1600shp Rolls Royce Gnome H 1400—1 free power turbines.
Rotor Diameter 62' 0" **Length** 54'9" **Height** 17'2" **Max Weight** 23,500lb **Max Speed** 120 knots.
The 3 versions are:-

AEW 2

Role: Airborne Early Warning. **Crew**: 1 pilot and 2 observers.
Avionics: Thorn/EMI searchwater radar. Marconi Orange Crop passive ESM equipment.
Armament: Nil.
Squadron Service: 849 HQ, 849A and 849B flights in commission.
Notes: Used to detect low flying aircraft trying to attack aircraft carrier battle groups under shipborne radar cover. Can also be used for surface search utilising its sophisticated, computerised long range radar. During 1988 849A flight will be embarked in HMS ILLUSTRIOUS and 849B in HMS ARK ROYAL. 849HQ acts as a training and trials unit at RNAS CULDROSE.

HAS 5

Roles: Anti-submarine search and strike. SAR. Transport.
Crew: 2 pilots, 1 observer and 1 aircrewman.
Avionics: MEL Sea Searcher radar; Plessey Type 195 variable depth active/passive sonar. GEC LAPADS passive sonobuoy analyses. Marconi Orange Crop passive ESM equipment.
Armament: 4 fuselage hardpoints capable of carrying STINGRAY, Mk 46/Mk 44 torpedoes or depth charges. Various flares, markers, grenades and sonobuoys can be carried internally and hand launched. A 7.62mm machine gun can be mounted in the doorway.
Squadron Service: 706, 810, 814, 819, 820, 824 and 826 squadrons in commission.
Notes: The SeaKing has been the backbone of the Fleet Air Arm's anti-submarine force since 1970. A further improved version, the HAS 6 is undergoing development. 706 is the advanced training squadron at RNAS CULDROSE. 810 is an operational training squadron with the capability to embark to reinforce the front line. During 1988, 814 squadron will be embarked in HMS ILLUSTRIOUS and 820 in HMS ARK ROYAL. 819 is shore based at PRESTWICK. 824 is a trials unit also based at HMS GANNET and 826 provides flights for service in RFA ships. The HAS 5 has a noteable SAR capability which is frequently demonstrated in the south west approaches.

HC 4

Role: Commando assault and utility transport.
Avionics: —
Crew: 1 pilot and 1 aircrewman.
Armament: Door mounted 7.62mm machine gun.
Squadron Service: 707, 845 and 846 squadrons in commission.
Notes: Capable of carrying up to 27 troops in the cabin or a wide variety of underslung loads up to 8,000lb in weight. 707 squadron is a training unit at RNAS YEOVILTON. 845 and 846 squadrons are based at YEOVILTON but able to embark or detach at short notice to support 3 Commando Brigade. The Sea King HC4 has a fixed undercarriage with no sponsons and no radome.

107

Westland LYNX

Variants: HAS 2, HAS 3
Roles: Surface search and strike; anti-submarine strike; SAR.
Engines: 2 x 900hp Rolls Royce GEM BS 360-07-26 free shaft turbines.
Rotor diameter: 42'0" **Length** 39'1¼" **Height** 11' 0" **Max Weight** 9,500lb.
Max Speed: 150 knots. **Crew**: 1 pilot and 1 observer.
Avionics: Ferranti SEA SPRAY radar. Marconi Orange Crop passive ESM equipment.
Armament: External pylons carry up to 4 x SEA SKUA air to surface missiles or 2 x STINGRAY, Mk 46 or Mk 44 torpedoes, depth charges, flares or markers.
Squadron Service: 702, 815 and 829 squadrons in commission.
Notes: 702 is a training squadron based at RNAS PORTLAND. 815, also based at Portland is the parent unit for single aircraft flights that embark in Type 42 destroyers and some classes of frigate, specialising in the surface strike role. 829 squadron parents flights in the Type 22 and other anti-submarine frigates. A version of the Lynx, the AH1, is operated by the Royal Marines Brigade Air Squadron which is based at RNAS Yeovilton.

Westland WASP HAS 1

Engine: 1 x 710shp Rolls Royce NIMBUS 103 free power turbine.
Crew: 1 pilot, 1 aircrewman and up to 3 passengers.
Notes: For years the Wasp was the standard helicopter carried by small ships. A few remain at sea parented by 829 squadron at RNAS PORTLAND but its replacement by the Lynx is almost complete and it is to be withdrawn from front line service in the near future. A few will remain on second line duties throughout 1988/89.

Westland GAZELLE HT2

Engine: 1 x 592shp Turbomeca ASTAZOU free power turbine.
Crew: 1 or 2 pilots.
Notes: In service with 705 squadron at RNAS CULDROSE. Used for training all RN helicopter pilots up to "wings standard" before they move onto the SeaKing or Lynx. A version of the Gazelle, the AH1, is used by the Royal Marines Brigade Air Squadron based at RNAS Yeovilton.

OTHER AIRCRAFT TYPES IN ROYAL NAVY SERVICE DURING 1988/89

British Aerospace JETSTREAM T2 and T3
Engines: 2 x 940hp Turbomeca ASTAZOU 16D turboprops. (T3 Garrett turboprops).
Crew: 1 or 2 pilots, 2 student observers plus 3 other seats.
Notes: A number of these aircraft are used by 750 squadron at RNAS CULDROSE for training Fleet Air Arm Observers.

de Havilland CHIPMUNK
Engine: 1 x 145hp de Havilland Gipsy Major 8 piston engine.
Crew: 2 pilots.
Notes: Used by the RN Flying Grading Flight at Roborough airport near Plymouth (and as such the first aircraft flown by generations of naval aircrew) and by stations flights at RNAS CULDROSE and YEOVILTON.

de Havilland SEA DEVON
Engines: 2 x 340hp de Havilland Gipsy Queen 70 piston engines.
Crew: 1 pilot, 1 aircrewman and up to 8 passengers.
Notes: 2 of these veteran transport aircraft remain as part of 771 squadron at RNAS CULDROSE.

de Havilland SEA HERON
Engines: 4 x 250hp de Havilland Gipsy Queen 30 piston engines.
Crew: 1 pilot, 1 aircrewman and up to 12 passengers.
Notes: In service since 1961, 4 of these excellent work horses remain in the station flight at RNAS YEOVILTON. They provide an inter-air station clipper service and support front line units with stores and transport.

British Aerospace CANBERRA TT18
Engines: 2 x 6500lb thrust Rolls Royce AVON turbojets.
Crew: 1 pilot and 1 observer.
Notes: Used by the (civilian manned) Fleet Requirements and Aircraft Direction Unit (FRADU) at RNAS YEOVILTON. Canberras provide towed targets for live firings by ships at sea.

Hawker HUNTER T8 and GA11
Engine: 1 x 7575lb thrust Rolls Royce AVON turbojet.
Crew: T8 1 or 2 pilots. GA11 1 pilot.
Notes: The Royal Navy has used Hunters to train fixed wing pilots since 1958. A number remain in service at RNAS YEOVILTON with the RN flying standards flight and with FRADU who use them as airborne targets for the aircraft direction school.

Westland WESSEX HU5
Engines: 2 x Rolls Royce GNOME free power turbines.
Crew: 1 or 2 pilots, 1 aircrewman and up to 12 passengers.
Notes: Now replaced in the commando assault role by the Seaking HC4. A handful of Wessex remain in service for fleet requirements duties.

In addition to these aircraft, the following aircraft have naval functions:
CANBERRA T17: Used by 360 joint RN/RAF squadron for electronic warfare tasks. Based at RAF WYTON.
British Aerospace 125: Two aircraft, owned by the RN are operated by RN aircrew as part of 32 squadron RAF based at RAF NORTHOLT.
The Fleet Air Arm Historic flight based at RNAS YEOVILTON has a **SWORDFISH, SEAHAWK, SEAFURY, FIREFLY and TIGER MOTH** on strength and these are often seen at air displays in the summer months.

Full details of these and many other naval aircraft can be found in the new and completely revised edition of AIRCRAFT OF THE ROYAL NAVY SINCE 1945 published by Maritime Books..

At the end of the line . . .

Readers may well find other warships afloat which are not
mentioned in this book. The majority have fulfilled a long and
useful life and are now relegated to non-seagoing duties. The
following list gives details of their current duties:

Penn. No.	Ship	Remarks
A191	BERRY HEAD	Maintenance Ship. Used as an Accommodation Ship at Devonport
C35	BELFAST	World War II Cruiser Museum ship—Pool of London (Open to the public)
D73	CAVALIER	World War II Destroyer. Museum Ship at Hebburn. Awaiting restoration.
D12	KENT	County Class Destroyer—Sea Cadet Training Ship at Portsmouth
F39	NAIAD	Static Trials Vessel—Portsmouth
F108 F113	LONDONDERRY FALMOUTH	Type 12 Frigates Harbour Training Ships—Gosport
S11	ORPHEUS	Oberon Class Submarine Harbour Training Ship at Gosport
S67	ALLIANCE	Submarine Museum Ship at Gosport (Open to the public)

**At the time of publishing the following ships were awaiting tow
for scrap or sale.**

PORTSMOUTH
Rame Head
Finwhale
Sealion
Wakeful
Ashanti
Galatea
Leander

Aurora
Alfriston
Bickington
Hodgeston
Bildeston
Bossington
Stubbington

**MILFORD
HAVEN**
Eskimo
Woodlark
(Targets)

ROSYTH
Dreadnought
Lofoten
Stalker

PLYMOUTH
Ajax